"*Cracked Pot* is a soul-baring memoir of love, creativity, loss, grief, and creativity again. Sentence by beautifully wrought, thoughtful sentence, Vince Montague narrates the premature death of his wife, Julia, and how he was able to rebuild his life by way of the clay and kilns and inspiration she left behind for him."
—Benjamin Dreyer, *New York Times* bestselling author of *Dreyer's English*

"If you've somehow lost your heart in the fog of grieving, your hands might just provide a roadmap to rediscovery. Vince Montague's *Cracked Pot* arrives from a chasm of emptiness, building with profundity and grace upward to a quiet roar."
—Bruce Dehnert, co-author of the bestseller *Simon Leach's Pottery Handbook*, master kiln-builder, artist, and member of the International Academy of Ceramics (UNESCO)

"Vince Montague's *Cracked Pot* is a wondrous memoir of personal reinvention and the transformative power of art.... This volume, like finely wrought ceramics, is something beautiful you can hold in hand and treasure always."
—Roy Parvin, author of *In the Snow Forest* and *The Loneliest Road in America*

"*Cracked Pot* resonates with its multiple meanings and meditates on love and death from title to the last word. This is raw life, raw materials, raw feelings, salvaged by the silken slip of clay, the discovery of thinking with your hands."
—Maw Shein Win, author of *Storage Unit for the Spirit House*

CRACKED POT

Cracked Pot

For permissions, contact: editor@latahbooks.com

Book and cover design by Kevin Breen

ISBN: 978-1-957607-09-2
Cataloging-in-Publication Data is available upon request

Manufactured in the United States of America

Published by Latah Books
www.latahbooks.com

The author may be contacted at vince.montague@gmail.com

CRACKED POT

A Memoir

Vince Montague

Preface

Pottery is made from clay and other raw materials. Clay is a transformational substance, a mixture of elements bonded together. It is dug from the earth and formed (the wet state), trimmed and glazed (the dry state), and ultimately fired to a high temperature until hardened (the solid state).

Grief is holding a porcelain bowl in the palms of one's hands, fingers slipping, grip loosening, bowl cascading, universe shattering, consciousness bracing against the certainty of death.

A grief junkie is someone who won't accept the notion of forgetting, a person who immediately attempts to retrieve the broken shards of the porcelain bowl in an effort to reconstruct the fractured clay, chunk by chunk, chip by chip, shard by shard.

THE WET STATE

Definition: The Wet State

The most plastic state; malleable and responsive; the moment when clay feels most adaptable; the platform with the most potential for growth and yet the greatest danger for failure. It includes the territory of courage, invention, and play; a youthful state, a place of ignorance, a house of freedom.

Beginnings

My wife Julia is instructing me how to roll coils and then pinch the clay into the shape of a vessel. *Just make a bowl,* she says. It sounds so simple. She hands me some clay and creates space on her worktable. Julia is busy producing pots for a pit fire later in the month and suggests I make something. Since I am going to be helping her fire the pit, it is reasonable to put something of my own inside.

Julia is a professional potter. I help her with her pottery business—carrying boxes, cleaning shelves, moving pots—but I've never worked with clay. I've never made something with my hands. I hesitate at first because, in my mind, clay belongs to her. Ceramics is her domain as an artist. Julia doesn't see things that way, but I do. The last thing I would ever want would be to spoil someone's art space, so I'm cautious while she is open. This is the advantage of being married to someone like-minded, free-spirited, someone who understands how much it takes to create art but also sees art as an invitation.

Julia demonstrates how to make a cup. *Don't think about it so much,* she says. *Just make a cup. Just make a bowl.* All right. I'll go along. I pinch several pots inside her studio and, after a time, find myself quietly involved with the clay. All those thoughts about invading her space and creating tension vanish. We say very little and simply work side by side. We listen to music from a playlist I've never heard, instruments unknown to me. What a joy to listen to music as I work. "Where is this from?" I ask, but I don't catch the name; I'm too distracted by the clay. Julia completes her work on her wheel, the pots flowing through her hands with ease. She cleans up and leaves to make dinner.

I love my wife because she doesn't take things as seriously as me. She is someone who doesn't believe in holding back; art streams through her every action. You can love someone because of the way they make you see the world, how they bring you to a place you would have never discovered all on your own. I continue to work, lost in the pursuit of forming shapes. This is the first experience where my hands mold clay, and the moment feels like a gift to me. I make a small bowl, cover it in plastic to keep it wet, and then join my wife for dinner. Beyond the deck, a deer in the woods stares back at me.

Six months later, Julia will be gone from my life forever.

Supplies

If I could explain how I came to work with clay, I'd betray the mystery and inherent wisdom of dirt. What happened was this: Instead of running away and losing myself in forgetting, I allowed the mystery of clay into my life and agreed to follow wherever it led me. And while there's nothing wrong with forgetting or pretending not to care about what's missing in one's life, that kind of strategy eventually runs out of steam and ends badly. The important thing is to find a way to survive, however you can.

How to survive? Look at the clues that surround us. For example, every pot pulled from the kiln has a story to tell, one of them being the story of its own survival. Pick up a pot and inspect it. Turn the pot upside down. Hold it with both hands. You'll discover clues as to where the pot was formed on the wheel, where it was trimmed, touched, held and impressed upon by the potter's intention. There are marks from the heat, tiny cracks from exposure to sudden cold. In the same way, I rise out of bed in the morning, hear the sound of my breath, feel the warmth of the bed, the ache in the stoop of my back; I see the creases on my face in the mirror, the graying hair on my arms. We bear the scars of our own endurance.

At a certain point, my interest in pots consumes me, overtakes my imagination, and I fall in love. The relationship doesn't happen overnight, but quietly over time, two decades after falling in love with a potter and then losing her suddenly and irrevocably in a tragedy. How to survive that kind of rupture? I took what I lost and invested that feeling into pots: looking at pots, drawing pots, holding pots, talking about pots, and eventually, miraculously, surprisingly—making pots of my own. At times my relationship with pots feels like the obsession of romantic love, the spark of meeting someone whose presence alters your own chemical constitution, a state of obsession when you wander back into your life consumed with that person, the touch of her hand, the curve of her back, the sound of her voice.

Wheel

Good to begin at the beginning, and yet when you think of your life in terms of the round, the bowl, the cylinder, beginnings and endings become one and the same. I rise each day from bed and pitch myself towards the clay studio to write the story of my life in pots: every cup a poem, every bowl a sprig of philosophy, and every teapot a story. All thoughts eventually come around again. I return precisely to where I finished the previous day. In the end, every cycle in the studio creates its own saga. Every kiln-load of pots writes its own history. I could tell you the story of my life if I could throw you a pot.

Metaphor

When I taught college writing, I confessed to my students that I was a failure as a writer, that I had written three novels and all of them were terrible. I confessed this information because it was true and because I felt if I were going to teach them to be writers, they had to understand from the beginning that writing wasn't easy for most people. Just because I was standing before them as an instructor, they shouldn't infer that I was a master at writing and language. All I could offer was my honesty and my experience. When it came to the mechanics of writing, I was sloppy and careless. I wasn't proud of being this way, I told them. I'd been fighting this fight against my own laziness my whole life; writing sentences was just one of the battlefields where I tried to improve myself. What we all should care about is the content and meaning, the thoughts we want to express, and following a set of grammatical rules aids communication, makes it easier for people to understand what we're thinking. This is what I said to my students. I'm not sure if they were actually listening.

One day a student asked me a question during an unfortunate detour about the use of similes, analogies, and metaphor. She asked: Why do we have to compare? Why do we need these tools? Why can't we state what we mean directly? It was a good question, one for which I didn't have the answer except my own honesty. I replied that I was simply teaching the rules, this was the chapter where the syllabus said we should be, that all of these rules offered us tools. But I also added that being direct wasn't always the best approach to understanding and knowledge, as counterintuitive as that might sound. The brain absorbs how it can absorb. We can't simply look up the answers in the back of a mathematics book and claim to understand calculus. Knowing the answer or making a direct statement doesn't necessarily communicate its meaning. Sometimes you need to find a sideways door. Sometimes we need to bend and stretch the imagination in order to communicate.

Here is all I can say: there are mornings when I wake up as a widower and I feel nuclear, as if I'm radiating a flood of energy into the world, but it's invisible, non-material. When I say I wake up and feel "nuclear," I don't mean that I am a nuclear bomb, but the reference to a nuclear bomb gets closer to my meaning, for which I have no words to directly employ.

Seven

The night my life changes, the skies drizzle rain.

I still think about that period of several hours and how our worlds separated on that evening, going over in my mind what I was doing while the truck was hauled from the water, her body retrieved before being taken to the coroner's. What was I doing? I've lost the specific memory, but probably just the same mundane tasks I always had done, my last two hours of innocence in the world filled with checking email, grading student papers, checking sport scores. Just filler.

The computer is all-encompassing when teaching in the online environment. I am new and appreciative of the freedom it gives me to step outside the physical classroom. There are scheduled tasks that I have to complete by midnight, and I am engulfed when I hear a knock on my door. Never does anyone come to our front door and knock, but I see through the windows that there is someone out there, a uniformed man whom I don't recognize.

What is going through my head? What are the signs I've missed? I remember thinking about food, about what to eat, but nothing else except opening the door and seeing the county sheriff, his badge, and the rotating red and blue lights of his vehicle. I'm thinking this has to do with the two dogs I rescued earlier this afternoon, the dogs who appeared out of nowhere, barking at Julia's studio, running in circles until I calmed them. The officer asks me if I know Julia and what my relationship is with her. I reply that I'm her husband. My first thought is that Julia has been arrested. But no, I'm wrong. He informs me that several hours ago, Julia was in an automobile accident along the Navarro River. She did not survive.

I raise my hands in the air to stop it, to stop something pouring down on me, because the words are too incomprehensible.

My body vibrates and then goes numb. Would he tell me again what happened? Did "not survive" mean she died?

I pace back and forth, my hands clutching the sides of my head. I want to find her; I need to see her. The sheriff advises me to not go anywhere because it is dark, because the roads are still wet and because I am shaking. *I shouldn't get in a car right now, should I?* I wonder what I am supposed to do. I worry about Julia. *You mean, what?* I don't have enough gears to keep myself balanced. He asks me if there is someone I should call. Are there children? No, there are no children. He advises me to sit down and stop pacing back and forth. Some part of me has left my body. I check the clock; it is almost nine. She should have been home by seven.

The sheriff was not on the scene of the accident, but he was told by others that they believe Julia lost control of the steering during that early evening rainstorm; the truck hydroplaned, slipped over the riverbank, and submerged halfway beneath the surface. Water filled the interior. He explains to me that two drivers stopped their cars along the highway and swam into the river to try and break the window to rescue her. The emergency team reached the scene too late. When they arrived, they shot a hole in the windshield and eventually pulled her body toward the shore.

I'd never heard such a story, never in my life.

I ask, "Is there something I'm supposed to do?" How insane I must sound to inquire if there are rules or procedures to follow in the event of a drowning. How insane I am to imagine logic existed, as if hope survived, or as if politeness and following rules could return Julia's life.

"No," the sheriff says, "there's nothing."

That is probably the moment. I sit down on the porch steps. My phone starts ringing.

Stuttering

Having no explanations for her death, I accept the unknown as the only truth which bears understanding. My new world now runs on reverse logic. Confusion offers tranquility. Uncertainty makes my blood flow. The gray hues of doubt tingle the hairs on my forearms. I know for certain there is truth hidden inside a landscape of ignorance.

Perhaps the shock will never wear off; perhaps I'll feel adrenalized every day for the rest of my life. I am at the sheriff's department to pick up some items retrieved from our truck hauled from the river and towed to the local dump. The county jail and the sheriff's office are one and the same, so I talk through bulletproof glass.

"I'm here to pick up a package," I say.

"For whom?"

"For m-m-m-e," I say. Even simple questions can flummox. I show my driver's license. While I wait, I'm looking through the plated glass into the office of desks, searching for the sheriff who drove up to my house and informed me my wife was dead. His face has made an indelible print on my imagination, and the writer in me wonders what kind of job it must be to give news like that to the unsuspecting. An administrative officer pushes a yellow manila envelope under the glass and then turns away.

"Have a good day," he says.

Outside in the parking lot, I lean against my car. I'd imagined there to be some type of box, not a yellow envelope, but all right. At least it's something. I open the envelope to discover Julia's wallet with all her identification, her credit cards, pictures of us, some cash. These are the items that remain from the truck. Her wallet is still soaking wet.

It takes me a moment in the slurry of my brain. I know Julia fought to get out of the truck; I also know she'd feared water. I remember when we were dating, she told me that she didn't think she would live a long life and sometimes that scared her. I think to myself: I should have accompanied her that day; I should have taken the ride to the coast and taken a day off. Instead, I wanted time to write.

I walk around the jailhouse and smoke a cigarette. I don't know what I can do to stop this pain in me. I can't imagine how I am supposed to live.

Turkey vultures circle overhead, and the crusted limbs of fallen oak trees lay along the hillside. My life incinerates, vanishing day after day, week after week. Where is Julia? What happened to her? I remain in a state of shock. I can't finish a sentence. When I speak on the phone, I stutter, thoughts bombarding my tongue at a rate that clutters and clogs my speech.

Maybe there exists, I think to myself outside the county jail, an in-between world, a waiting station of some sort where myself and Julia both live, not quite alive, and yet not quite dead. I feel at times that as I walk around this world—a world that looks so familiar to my old world—that Julia too is walking around in some other world, some place that might even look familiar to this one, and yet we are lost.

Desk

From my writing desk, I sit down to gather myself, to center my world as I usually do by writing in a notebook, making observations, drafting ideas for stories. My desk has been my solace in life. By instinct and by routine, I sit down to write.

But everything is different now. I sit, but I cannot write. I have no interest in writing. The pages appear pathetic and formless. My notebooks are full of notes transcribed just days before Julia died, notes from my own imagination. My scribbles and attempts at prose appear superficial and reveal my lazy thinking. I re-read what I have written, feel embarrassed for myself, the ignorance, the stupidity of writing and thinking the world has a certain shape to it, one that conforms by employing ideas into words.

Inside a box underneath my desk are old journals. How many are there? How long have I indulged this habit? I open one and begin to read, and once I start it is impossible to cease. I feel like a detective searching for clues, trying to make a rough sketch of this person who is me or who was once me. I read and re-read these old notebooks, looking for triggers of memory, signs of life, but my words camouflage, even in my notebooks. The pain is too sharp, the reminders of someone who no longer exists. That part of me is dead; I am no longer a writer. That part of me that wrote in journals and loved literature died in the truck with Julia.

I am swimming in the ocean at night, the dark all around me, holding my breath while diving underwater, coming up for air, and then going back down, the water temperature the same as the air. There is darkness and fear surrounding me, and like now, there is a sense of everything under one roof, a closeness that makes my blood flow, my adrenaline flash.

Tonight I notice there is no moon at my desk, no light, just blinking clocks that display the incorrect time. Starlight bores pinholes through the sky like molecules under a microscope, the blurred brightness of another life.

Insanity

Grief is a type of craziness, controlled and stressful. You're not of your own mind at all. It's more than just feeling sad about a loss; grief unmasks the deception all around us, everyone pretending they own all the time in the world, as if somehow they're immune to extinction. Grief carves a separation between you and the rest of the world. The craziness sets in with grief when you feel like the only person who can see that kind of deception and yet you can't really say anything or do anything because this is how normal people live and your body wants to heal itself, your broken life desires to bring itself back into the mainstream, but you can't, because it's all so false and you think you're losing your mind.

Forgetting

After the memorial service, after the friends return to their lives, after the overflow of grief and disbelief, I come upon a different emptiness, a silent hollowness that begins a process of erasure. Like the sudden quiet after a turbulent storm, the normal din of ordinary life returns. Tragedy is just another blip on the screen. The days unfold with constant emptiness. Holidays arrive. Graduations. Fruit trees blossoming. It's time to file taxes. A conveyor belt of experience that won't stop and wait. The enemy becomes the daily act of forgetting while moving forward. In fact, the very thing that heals (time) is also the fuel for forgetting and deletion.

Here is where the next stage of grief begins, this empty space of bewilderment and the dynamic change of space fueled by loss. Unable to sleep in our bed, I lie on the living room floor in a sleeping bag listening to the owls in the oaks. The skies remain dark, close to dawn, when I hear a rustling of deer on the hill outside my window. All night long, creatures wander around the perimeter, signs of life creeping around just before sunrise.

Local potters inquire if I want to sell part of Julia's studio, her equipment, her tools, her clay, her kilns. Their timing strikes me as too swift, but later I realize this is how the world moves forward: commerce is commerce, resources are resources, everything becomes compost. In a way, maybe this predatory post-environment is a natural process to help me lighten my burden. It's just overwhelming to deal with these issues, so I decline their offers. I'm not ready.

One evening I have no place to go, nowhere to run. I walk into Julia's clay studio and flip on the lights. The sound of the door, the burst of light—all these sensations are familiar. I turn on the local radio and let the room fill with the sounds of other voices. I stand there for a moment, then turn off the radio, flip the lights and leave.

Making

Throwing pots is a method of manipulating the material of the earth to form a pot, but also the process of understanding how to inhabit the world where the pot is used. Handmade objects feel like energy points of light that dot our material world. When we make objects, we communicate with this invisible realm, we dialogue with the unsaid.

My adult years have been spent living alongside and using objects because I was married to a woman who created handmade pots and weaved them into our life. These pinched, coiled, thrown, and altered pots appeared lost and anachronistic in the larger context of our increasingly digital outer world, yet at the same time, courageous and bold. Pots charmed me for their resilience, their directness, their beauty. The feeling of holding a pot and using it with my hands felt electric and life-affirming. However, the notion that I could throw pots never entered the equation. I was a writer and a teacher; I worked using my mind and language to instruct students how to think and express their opinions in words. I wasn't someone who understood how to use tools or get my hands dirty.

Now I see how little I understood. Throwing pots is a commitment to an alternative perspective, a step beyond the world we typically navigate. Throwing pots aligns ourselves on the outer margins of an invisible realm so transforming yet so self-effacing and subtle we often forget: the territory of our hands, the gift of touch, the mystery of making with our own bodies.

Group

On Tuesday evenings, I meet with a group of individuals who have suffered recent traumatic loss. The others in the group have lost spouses or children, sisters or brothers. What we all have in common is the sudden trauma, most of it gruesome in the specifics, the details that make our grief unique. My wife has drowned. Her son has been killed. Her father was murdered. A couple lost their son to suicide. We are members of the population who have very little hope in the world, but somehow we remain here, bewildered and alone.

We gather in the living room of an old house in Santa Rosa with a leader from the local hospice. We listen to each other's stories and then take a break to have coffee or tea. It is during these times we learn how to normalize, how to be social, how to make a joke because we are in the company of others like ourselves, the mangled, the dribbled, the grief-stricken. For the first time, I find people I have something in common with, people who can understand me. The feeling shoots through me like a drug. I arrive early before our meetings and smoke cigarette after cigarette in the parking lot, thinking about what I am going to say and how I am going to say it.

Each week we have a project. Write a letter to your loved one. Make a collage from pictures from a magazine that describes your life together. We present these projects to each other. We Scotch-tape them on cardboard paper or adhere them with Elmer's glue. These projects feel like clichés, the work of grade-schoolers, the newly born, but they are effective. At the end of the six weeks, we move back into our own lives, not cured but more aware of what befalls us.

The final project is to write a letter to ourselves a year from now. Our hospice leader makes us write our address on an envelope, and then she collects our letters.

"Remember," says the hospice leader as I leave, "to eat and to sleep."

A year later, I retrieve my mail at the post office, and as I leave the building I see an envelope with my name on it, written in my handwriting. Walking through the parking lot, I am preoccupied and not paying close attention. Perhaps this envelope is a rejection letter from a publication, maybe it's a returned letter, but I am wrong. The letter is from me, the letter from a year ago, and it is not a rejection but an inquiry. I open the envelope inside my car.

Dear me, I wrote, *I wonder if you are still alive.*

Inheritance

Julia's clay studio is a building about the size of a single-car garage, but with skylights and a pair of hanging barn doors that part ways and open up to a cement kiln pad. It's surrounded by oaks and sits atop a small edge overlooking a narrow view into the valley below. In the center of the studio sits a wide table for hand-building, a way of working with clay without using a wheel. Her walls are covered with postcards, images of pottery, inspirations by other artists and sculptors. Colored lanterns hang from one end of the studio to the other. Drawings of pots, her handwritten notes to herself, glaze recipes, her music queued.

Every day I open up her studio, walk inside, make sure everything is the same, touch some of her finished pots (work scheduled for one gallery, other work for a commission, customers waiting), look around, and then leave. Today is different because I feel a bit stronger. Occasionally, I feel a burst of my old self. I find a mop and fill a bucket with water and get to work cleaning up. Working, moving my body, physical exertion—all of it pushes me temporarily out of the pain of grief.

I'm forty-seven years old and alone for the first time in over twenty years. Facing me are decisions about a future I can't even imagine, but I'm here now in Julia's studio, and I have some energy to wipe down the counters, to organize the bags of clay, to take out the garbage.

What's worse? Living next to a cemetery or making pots inside a cemetery? I'm afraid of the potency of her abandoned studio, unsure what to do with this space, how to live with it, how to live beside it, or if I should flee and save myself the pain. Everything in Julia's studio exists as a mystery to me, aftershocks of her death: her tools, her notes on firings, her work in progress, buckets and buckets of glaze, a snapshot of her life midstream, her work from wheel to kiln, her energy moving through the air with every breeze. The path of our actions in the world is the trace we leave behind.

I recall a strategy Julia and I employed when we got into disagreements. One evening we argued over money, over our lack of it, trying to figure out ways to do something other than blaming the other, so we agreed to leave the argument where it was, to retreat to our corners and to make art. We both had work to do. For Julia, to make pots; for me, to write. I resented carrying such a heavy teaching load; she resented the pressure to sell more work. We joked that we sometimes wished the other worked as an engineer or a lawyer, someone with a real salary, but the truth was the opposite. What we shared was art, and art was the bridge that resolved most problems.

I search among her materials and find a bag of clay. On her worktable, I create a space. I remember that first lesson Julia taught me a couple of months before she died. *Just make a bowl.*

Just make a cup. I find a bucket and fill it with water. There's a pile of towels underneath her worktable. My hands shake. I roll out coils on her table. Fuck it all, I'm thinking to myself. My head rushes with an idea to make another bowl, to make a set of bowls. Fuck everything. It doesn't matter what I do or what I don't do. The world is unlivable, unsurvivable, and impossible.

At a certain point I have to stop because I don't know how to move forward. A sphere of clay shaped and formed by my hands sits on the worktable. I close the studio and go for a walk.

Tools

A sponge.

An apron.

A bucket.

A pair of hands.

An old towel.

A pair of comfortable shoes.

A sense of wonder.

Gloves.

An open mind.

An appreciation for improvisation.

A knife.

Wedging

There is a truth that awaits us. Maybe it's a type of wisdom, a fullness of our experience, a birthright of our consciousness, but I believe that is what we seek when we make art. It's not just a cup. It's not just a bowl. It's the impulse to make with our hands that propels us beyond the physical plane.

Before I begin, it is necessary to wedge the clay. Wedging clay can look similar to what a baker does to knead dough, but in this case, wedging is about eliminating air bubbles, lining up the molecules inside the clay and preparing them to be manipulated. Wedging is the moment of contact, the first stage in the transformation of the particles within the clay and within me. I think of wedging as a rapprochement with the earth itself.

Often I wedge in haste, rushing and pushing, kneading the clay through my hands, shoving my palms downward like it's a race to wedge and unstiffen when it's not a race at all. Quickly I am stopped, however; the clay transforms everything into slow motion, ripens a softening in my hands, and embraces my grip with walls made of mud. Time lengthens, I slow down, I hear my breath, I notice the light beaming through the window. Thirty seconds can feel like thirty minutes. The clay knows how to handle someone like me, how to turn down the volume in my head and quiet my thoughts.

While I wedge, I consider what I'm going to do with the lump of clay before me and all of its endless possibilities. I could make a batter bowl. I could make an urn. I could make a plate for serving. Sometimes I don't know what kind of pot to make, so I just keep wedging the clay until I figure it out. Wedging is an excuse to dream, an exercise in drafting ideas and opening the imagination to play. After a time, my neck and shoulders relax.

Labyrinth

Monday begins with drifting clouds. I'm awake at sunrise, still shocked to recall Julia dead, my life in crisis. I turn my head to the windows to witness the magnificence of hammerhead clouds migrating south along the horizon. Every morning of my life seems impossible. My bloodstream still floods with drugs to help me sleep and relax. Now, a whole day waiting for me once I rise out of bed. If I can get off the floor. If I can attempt another day. That is how exhaustive grief can feel, just the physical weight of it. Like this morning waking up alone on my living room floor: auburn light, crinkled leaves, shortened days, clouds like worlds leaving me. It's too beautiful to move.

On Tuesday, I stop in a shopping mall to buy new bed sheets because our bed is no longer the same. I can't continue to sleep on the living room floor in my sleeping bag like a dog guarding a gate, but neither can I lie in our bed and feel the empty space. The smell of her remains, her touch, her sound. I can't absorb what I have lost, but neither can I withstand the small details, the tactile moments, the sensations of her alive when I am trying to accept her loss: the pillows cast in the shape of Julia's head, the hollow of her hips in the dip of the mattress, the restlessness of her body in the kicked sheets balled in the corner.

At the moment, grief makes everything seem reasonable, even something mundane like shopping. Perhaps it's fatigue after my first day back at my teaching job, my attempt to return to "normal." That is part of the reason, I'm sure, because my resistance is down. The other reason is more abstract. What awaits me at home is an empty house, a darkened bedroom, an engulfing silence. Going to work doesn't change the basic facts. Returning home to an empty space is the problem.

I signal, then take the exit off the freeway to find my way to a mall. The black cement of the parking lot feels strangely comforting to me, but then again I have always found refuge in parking lots. I disappear into a row of cars, each vehicle wrapped in brushed steel, darkened windows, corporate insignias. The light falls over Santa Rosa. Inside, I take an escalator to the second floor, and I recall coming here to buy a pair of pants to wear to Julia's memorial service a few months ago. Pieces of me continue to peel off, randomly disappearing. Farewell to the old me. Safe travels to the person I used to inhabit. Now I numb myself by looking at pillowcases and fitted sheets, wondering how I got here. I keep walking and walking the aisles, going in circles. I see how people might become addicted to the bright lights, the background music, the merry-go-round feeling that propels me from one department to another. Eventually, however, the store announces that it is time to close.

The parking lot is now mostly empty. I sit in my car and let it warm up. Out-of-date Christmas decorations gleam against the darkness.

Memory

I have heard that clay has "memory." The idea is that clay remembers where it came from, the minerals invested in itself, and how it was manipulated to arrive here on the potter's table. So, for example, when a round pot is taken off the throwing wheel and altered into something such as a square or rectangle, there exists in the expression of the clay a recollection of its previous shape, its former "roundness." And within that memory of clay lives a yearning desire to return to its original form.

I've always loved this idea, that somewhere within the molecules of clay there exists a consciousness of itself and its own history, a memory of its origin, an empathy with its history, an intelligence beyond our own. Indeed, there is a relationship of some sort between the artist and the material, the potter and the clay, an energy that's dynamic, full of possibility, and at the same time, possessed of guilt.

Clairvoyant

I am in the dining room of my friend's house in San Francisco. He has arranged for me to speak with a clairvoyant, somebody who speaks with the other side. I have brought with me one of Julia's mugs. We sit down, and I pass the mug to him.

I have never been to a clairvoyant. I have never had my tarot cards read. I've never been keenly interested in metaphysics, the occult, the mystical. I was raised in a Catholic family, schooled in cults and high levels of brainwashing from nuns and priests. I feel a natural resistance to anything spiritual or mystical. That's partially the trauma of a parochial youth and partially the product of teaching writing and working with facts and logic. In some back room of my mind, I looked down on all things psychic.

But now, everything is different.

I sit down at the table. The silence is palpable. My imagination wanders, and I begin to think that Julia is in this room, that she's been waiting for me, searching for me. Why should I be skeptical of things that can't be proven? I'm hunting to find Julia. I don't know where she's gone. I have to believe that there's a solution outside this physical world.

"How do you feel?" the clairvoyant asks me. I've met him before, but not in this context. He's a friend of my friend who arranged this meeting.

I tell him I'm nervous. I tell him I'm grateful to see him.

"She is with us," he says, and I want to believe him.

I want to believe Julia is with me right now, I really do, but I know the truth is otherwise. What I really want to know is whether or not Julia is all right, if she's safe, if she's stopped feeling pain. That's my worry and concern. I close my eyes to concentrate, listening to the ticking of a clock in a nearby room.

Breakage

Within the lifespan of a pot exists the ever-present threat of ruin, tragedy, and pain. Disaster spares not the smallest plate. Take, for example, the espresso cup, the delicate handle, the pouty lip. Consider the saucer held beneath, the suddenness of the snapping of a shoelace, the loss of balance. One day you'll forget your own space, twist your torso, and elbow your espresso toward the cement. There's no grace in disputing gravity. Instead, make everything into art, jewels of sorrow that shine in the mud. Bend down on your knees and study the shards. The truth resides in the mistakes, the borders trespassed, the losses that widen the gaps.

Relief

The greatest hurdle is understanding time. The more time passes, the farther removed from the person you've lost. And yet a sudden loss clutches you inside the present; remembering the past is too painful, speculating on the future impossible. So there is a compulsion to seize the moment because you know for a fact how fragile each moment is.

You have no control over time, and you never did. Grief makes it abundantly clear that time moves past you regardless. But the dynamic of time becomes exaggerated when you go through sudden loss. You live inside a paradox where the only thing that will heal you is the passage of time, and yet the movement of time and the absence you sense is the dagger that hurts the most.

Which is to say that each person who confronts a traumatic loss will then come face to face with a spiritual and spatial dilemma: where did the lost person go? Where did Julia travel after she died? Where am I going? Will we ever see each other again? I started to think that Julia didn't die, that she had moved to another room, another sphere. I could feel her pain as if she were close to me. Her confusion was like my confusion, as if we shared a wall in opposite rooms inside an empty house. That was me. That was how I saw my dilemma.

When death arrives, you have only your instincts to rely upon, your own mind on which this weighs so heavily. Maybe it will come suddenly. Maybe it will happen over time. Maybe your religious belief will soften the blow. Maybe it won't. I won't say there is any particular way to experience grief, a particular method to handle it best. The method you use is the one that helps you survive.

For me, I had started a pot of my own in Julia's studio. Of all the things weighing on my mind, the fate of that little bowl gave me hope. The following morning, I came back to check on its progress. From a distance, the bowl looked as if it had been kicked on its side. The interior was dented. The work recalled that of a child. I saw that the bowl could possibly hold something—water, soup, or maybe nothing, just itself. The bowl leaned to the right, a mess of clay, but it was the best I could do. For a few minutes, my mind engaged with something other than me and the trouble I was in.

Awkwardness

I sign up for a class in a pottery cooperative where Julia used to work. I know many of the people there who are potters, the professionals and weekend potters. It feels good to walk into the clay studio, but it seems as if everyone is watching me because the pain I carry is public. Everyone seems to know what happened to Julia. When her friend Randy sees me in the studio, he frowns.

"What's wrong?" I ask.

He doesn't say anything, but it is the sight of me, the recollection of the loss of Julia that makes him sad when we meet. This type of awkwardness happens more frequently, and I find myself having to manage the grief of others as well as my own. Randy hugs me. He tells me that he's been having dreams about Julia, that she's been speaking to him to keep making pots.

I believe Randy, but I don't know what to say, how to react. I know Julia's energy continues to flow through the atmosphere of the world, particularly clay.

Another one of Julia's friends sees me in the community studio and says hello. We go back and forth in small talk.

"It's great to see you working in clay," Emily says. This is the part where it becomes awkward because we have not mentioned Julia's death. For her part, Emily feels unsure of bringing it up with me. We are going along and having a conversation as if the world is a normal place where nothing happens but small talk.

"Yes," I say, "I think Julia would be shocked to see me attempting to wedge clay."

Now, the tension is released. I have broken the ice and mentioned the unmentionable. I discover most people to be fearful and hesitant. At first, I am surprised, but I realize later that every person has their own method of dealing with grief. No one knows what to say, or they're afraid of saying the wrong thing, the uncomfortable thing. Sometimes I just don't have the energy, and I find myself getting lost in the awkwardness and trying to enjoy it rather than be concerned.

Nothing could be worse than this, I say to myself. Nothing could be more tough.

Throwing

There are six of us in the beginning, and then two drop out. I haven't been a student in a classroom for more than twenty years, and I feel a deep relief not to be the one responsible for the lesson. How easy, I think, to simply show up, open my eyes, and listen. What a gift.

The class begins with a demonstration by the instructor. My brain beams in on the technique, the steps to be followed, the way to navigate. I try to absorb everything as best I can. I'd watched Julia throw hundreds of pots and I'd listened when she described what she was doing. Somewhere buried inside my brain is a second-hand knowledge, a background of throwing pots without having ever touched clay.

Still, I begin by anticipating disaster and working backwards to prevent it. When it is my turn, I take a pound of clay, get it spinning on the wheel, and then by the pressure applied by my hands, I lift the clay into the air.

Adrenaline

Truth of the matter is quite different. Be certain every attempt I try in the beginning fails. Rest assured, I am frustrated. My embarrassment increases as I observe the other students in the class making better progress. I note to myself that I shouldn't compare myself to others, but I always do, and clay is no different, unfortunately. I make several attempts on that first day of throwing. I imagine I'm not suited for clay. I step away from my wheel and go outside to smoke a cigarette. I return with new vigor. This time is even worse. I take my clay off the wheel and pretend to inspect my tools, as if the tools were the reason for my failure. With twenty minutes remaining in the class, the instructor approaches my wheel and assists me in centering the clay. She then shows me how to raise the walls of the pot. The class ends, and I cut off my new piece to dry, clean up my wheel, and walk out onto the street full of adrenaline with the belief of having thrown my first pot.

Chaperone

One of the things they neglect to tell you when you first start making pots is that in addition to making shapes, decorating them, and firing them, you're managing time. In fact, time is one of the tools you must employ.

Whereas time affected me in my real life and added to my grief, inside the clay studio I manipulated time as the clay moved from a wet state into a dry state and finally into a solid state. I am careful that the movement of time doesn't happen too quickly; I want the water to evaporate slowly so there will be no cracks, that attachments will adhere without falling off, that the clay and the glazes will vitrify at the right moments in the heat of the kiln. I cover my pots in my studio with bedsheets as if tucking them in for sleep. The fabric creates a tent over the work and slows the process of evaporation. There are all sorts of tricks to fool time, but make no mistake, time is always moving forward.

In order to do so, you have to escort your bowl as it navigates the process from wet to dry to solid. You can never really stop taking care of your bowl, and that means being conscious of time and where this bowl exists inside the course of time. So, in my mind I own timelines of each pot, each cup, each plate, thinking about them in the studio, just formed on the wheel, trimmed and drying on the rack, glazed and posted to fire. It's like taking care of a flock, ushering them through the passage of time, gently but with purpose.

Cart

Back home, the yard in front of Julia's kiln is lined with throwaways, the ceramic misfires, pots with runny glazes, chipped bottoms or cracked rims. This is the area where Julia discarded all the pottery mistakes, where shards and broken pots litter the landscape. At times, walking to the studio feels like navigating a natural disaster, plates and vases strewn against tree stumps and redwood benches, the aftermath of a hurricane.

And here, inside the studio and home gallery, packed in boxes or tucked on shelves, lives the pots of our friends, other potters, pots that are decades old, pots that never sold, pots that might be sold, pots that haven't moved for decades, pots that need repair, pots missing a lid, pots and more pots.

What's more strange is the debris of what might have been, the scattered notes that trickle in from the future. Julia's pots continue to sell; checks arrive in the mail from galleries that carry her work. People continue to use her bowls and cups.

I can mourn the physical, but there are other kinds of losses, and these can be the most profound. This evening, I walk over to Julia's studio along a trail of broken teapots and flip the lights. Her studio has taken on the character of a spaceship that has landed inside my life, a new geography to explore, a vessel that houses potential messages to absorb and understand. Here is a space that belonged to Julia, a place where she worked and applied her talents, a place I know little about. Here stands her throwing wheel, her tools, her towels. Here is her bucket and apron. Here is a notebook and her journal of her art. Here is where as much of her talent and hard work could fit into one space.

How unfortunate that most of us never know the full extent of our gifts to the world because a person's gifts aren't usually fully acknowledged until the person is dead and gone. And while it makes me sad, the energy and wisdom also inspires, gives me fuel to burn. I'm thinking about all the desire, all the ambition, all the passion and love that Julia had for making pots, and it's impossible to believe that this kind of energy can simply disappear.

For the first time, I take serious stock of Julia's entire studio. I have a better idea of what I'm looking at now, the essentials that are needed for clay. An art studio reads like a map of the artist's soul, and Julia was someone who loved having a lot of supplies. I see there is enough clay in the studio for me to last for several months, books for me to read about how to make pots, tools to use in order to create pots, a kiln to fire the pots. Everything in this studio is turnkey, ready to go.

My first problem sits in the rear of the studio, dusty and full of spider webs: two monolith ware carts, each about ten feet high and six feet long. They are made of metal and hold roughly thirty pots made by Julia, pots that have not been fired.

I can't pretend I haven't seen these pots. I can't ignore that I am picking up a glazed and unfired bowl that Julia made but died before she could complete. Part of me now understands that I can't leave these pots unfinished, that these pots are not like all the other pots that surround me. These pots need to be fully brought into the world.

But how? Who is going to fire these pots?

The only answer is me; I'm going to fire these pots, I say to myself. I'm going to fire this kiln again.

I know the kiln should be fully packed with pots in order for the load of pots to fire correctly and efficiently. Right now, there are not enough pots on the ware cart to fire a kiln. I am uncertain how I came to possess this knowledge that a kiln shouldn't be fired only half-full, whether I overhead Julia say something to this effect, or if someone had mentioned that detail and it stuck in my memory. It doesn't matter either way or if the information is true or false. The knowledge is passive and arrives from somewhere in my subconscious, like a note slid under a door at night.

Just make a bowl. Just make a cup.

Vehicles

Pots are vessels much like poems; both are vehicles of thought and feeling, bodies of containment. There are good poems and bad poems, good pots and bad pots. There is something in a poem that suggests a pot by its sturdiness and mystery. There is something in a pot that suggests a poem by the way the curve of the belly descends to the foot, for example.

I'm not saying all pots are poems, but they both come to me as the material of my life and so I meld them together. I make them one urge that pulses through me.

Studio

New thought this morning: everything that is tragedy can also be transformed into lark.

The goal becomes to make enough pots to fill the rest of the kiln. I am in search of any kind of motive to do anything, to get out of bed, to look forward to an oncoming day, to anticipate something new and fresh.

The fear of firing a kiln gives me energy. How am I going to pull this off? Where am I going to start? That's the drug, that's the buzz inside my head from grief; my body and mind crave this rush because grief has taken over my life and found its way into clay. It feels like being drunk, a simultaneous softening and heightening of perception that relieves the heart and somehow gives me the energy to live.

I have to take stock of myself. Is it possible to fire a kiln with only a few pottery lessons under my belt, a general awareness (but little skill) of how to fire a kiln? Normal logic would advise caution, but everything now reads backwards and upside down. Of course, I can fire a kiln. What is the opposite of caution? There is no need to take anything too seriously or to be scared of anything whatsoever.

I'm frustrated, however; it's a very complicated dance to

make a pot, a process that appears simple on the outside but is the result of hundreds upon hundreds upon hundreds of quick gestures and fast decisions. Learning how to throw pots is not something I can rush. Technique and hand skills take time and experience. When making a pot, there is ample opportunity to self-sabotage.

I'm here, now, on Julia's wheel, attempting for the fifth time this morning to throw a cylinder with a flat bottom and straight up and down sides, but I am having trouble just centering the clay on the wheel. The clay is too hard, and I can't control it. My arms tire. Five attempts and five duds, and then suddenly I'm spent. I have to admit throwing pots is discouraging in the beginning.

But discouragement feels like the new normal, and I don't seem to be bothered by it overall. What in the world, at some level, isn't discouraging? Maybe that is my experience because I am not a centered person at the moment; my energies spew in every direction, and everything I touch seems to tilt in the direction of ruin. I wake up feeling more cracked than the day before.

Likewise, every day in the studio is just another moment in disaster. There is so much to absorb inside the world of a clay studio. Everywhere I look I see more questions than answers: bags and bags of clay, buckets of tools, platters sitting on wooden bats, firing logs, unmarked buckets of unknown material, jars marked "Terra Sigiliata," a recipe for a glaze scribbled on a piece of paper: 2400 grams of Custer Feldspar.

I have never worked with my hands or done anything mechanical. I come from a family where the most we had to do mechanically was to mow the lawn. We weren't a rich family but a fearful one. To this day, I have no idea how an engine works. I've read a few books about carpentry, but I've only used a saw a few times in my life. I've assembled futon couches that never quite fit. I become discouraged when I enter hardware stores. I'm not proud of any of this, but I have to get over myself and learn how to use this material and these hundreds of tools if I want to keep this studio alive.

Curve

I am told the very thing you need to do when you begin throwing pots is to imagine the inside space of the pot.

I remember watching someone throw a pot on the wheel, and they spoke of the process as if building a house. After you center the clay, you have to open it up and create the floor of the pot. After you create the floor, you begin to raise the walls of the pot. So you have to know beforehand if you're going to have a curved floor or a straight perpendicular floor depending on what you dream of making. The curved bottom is the bowl. The straight walls are cylinders. Those are the two choices.

But you have to first imagine.

Then you have to suspend disbelief.

Julia

In 1986 I moved to New York to become a writer. I had ambitions to write stories and be an artist. I was broken as a human being, and that is why I came to New York and why I was positive I had to live there and be a writer. I was naive about my whole life, about being an artist, about everything, but that was me. My naiveté had gotten me to New York at the age of twenty-three with a winter coat that was really nothing more than a windbreaker. My naiveté protected me because I was oblivious to the dangers. All I knew was that every morning I woke up in New York I felt as if I had finally come home. I had finally found a place where I felt I belonged.

I lived in a space in the East Village, renting out the living room from an artist who worked with metals, torching and melding in her bedroom which doubled as her art studio. I had never lived with a woman as a roommate. I had never lived in a space where I couldn't close a door and be alone. But that was all right because I had somehow managed to leave California, move across the country, and manifest a life as a writer living in New York. The hardest part turned out to be writing.

And then one day I met a young woman seated next to me in a writing workshop. A pile of copies of a story she had written sat in front of her, copies to be handed out to the class. It was nerve-wracking to be in a graduate fiction workshop at NYU. The building on University Place felt trampled upon: a narrow staircase, tiny meeting rooms, worn carpets, fluorescent lighting, faded couches, the ambiance of a shady medical office. I felt over my head and beyond my capacities. How did I get in? But there I was with copies of my story in front of me. We were waiting for the class to begin, and I was feeling anxious, so I asked the woman sitting next to me if she had brought her story to the class. Julia turned to look at me. Then she turned and stared at her pile of stories on the table in front of her. Then she looked back at me and said nothing, sparkling with confidence and energy.

Weeks later, I was walking up West Broadway with a girl I had been dating. She was serious about me, but I wasn't feeling the same toward her. I was drifting around New York and couldn't be tied to anyone. I felt out of my head to be studying poetry, meeting writers, exploring art. This girl worked as an editorial assistant for a women's magazine in mid-town. She was rich and didn't worry about money or about having to survive in New York. I was a writer and didn't feel comfortable except as being a writer; being part of a couple didn't feel like something that could ever belong to me. I told her all I cared about was books and literature. I was just being honest. I made a lousy boyfriend because every fiber of me burns to be a writer.

On that night, I had just bought my first winter coat at Cheap Andy's. It was late autumn, and I was walking with this girl, knowing this relationship wouldn't last and yet having a good time, the air biting against my skin. The streets were both bright and dark, lots of neon, people moving fast, passing by shop windows. The days had become short, and my life began when the sun set. I never wore gloves or a hat because I still thought I was living in California, but I remember the sidewalks pulsing with people out on a Friday night and thinking that I really should get a hat when someone rushed me from behind and pressed her shoe down on the heel of my shoe. Then she ran away. There I am on West Broadway wearing one shoe. When I turned around, I saw Julia with a friend of hers, laughing and disappearing into the stream of humanity moving in the other direction.

Fantasy

I wedge and wedge like I am pumping life back into my ruined world. I want so much to turn back time and see Julia standing behind her pottery wheel. I can't avoid the memory of her throwing pots on her wheel, her hub of activity in the studio. I can't ignore her bucket of tools and stamps she made to impress on the clay. But especially, the wheel. I can't make it disappear because the wheel is integral to everything.

Denial is a useful medicine, until it isn't.

Resume

A few months after Julia's memorial service, her "celebration of life," I'm on my way to the classroom. I have gone back to teaching in the physical classroom as a way to fill my days, to normalize my life, to have contact with other people, to resume what remains of my gutted world. It makes sense to lose myself in teaching, to use my role as a teacher as a distraction and as a tool to hang on to what remains. This logic sounds rational, but the appearance of logic is a façade. A year later, and I still live in a world of insanity, the world of being a widower. Every minute defies normal logic. Where is Julia? Where has she disappeared to? I continue to absorb the idea that I will never see her again. Nobody wants to talk about that part of death. Nobody wants to talk to me about the irrational, the never-understood, the questions that have no answers.

I am walking Mission Street while planning inside my head a lesson for a class I will teach in twenty minutes to art students who want to learn how to write so they can market themselves better in the workplace. Teaching artists is the latest niche I have found as a writing instructor, but even now I procrastinate and put off preparing my classes until the last minute. I typically end up winging it about halfway through a class. This morning before coming to work, I was on the phone trying to cancel Julia's telephone account. I have finally taken the step of canceling her phone because previously it was the only way I could hear her voice. Now, I'm gearing myself up to teach how to write a resume, how to write about art, how to sell themselves as artists in the real world of commercial art.

I'm not a natural teacher, but I find that I can teach and overcome my shyness if I see a larger purpose. I don't really care that I am teaching them how to use "action" verbs or how to fashion a concluding statement in a cover letter. I care that I am helping someone find their skill in writing to help benefit themselves. And on whatever level, whether it be poetry or simply writing a letter to get a job, writing is a transformative tool. I have to create within my mind some sort of satisfaction, some sense of contribution to the world. But today I am crossing the entrance to the building and thinking to myself I can't possibly step into the classroom and teach students how to get a job in the marketplace as designers or animators or fine artists. I can't do it.

Now, I see everything differently.

The students drift in one by one and sit down. The seats fill. Students who haven't shown up in weeks suddenly appear. I scurry through notes on my desk. The walls turn from gray to white. I receive a message from the phone company wanting documented proof of Julia's death, a copy of the death certificate by the end of the day.

The class begins. I feel buggy-eyed and sweaty.

Resumes are personal documents, I say, an accounting of who you are and what you've done. The students stare back at me, wishing that I would stop talking and just give them a template they can copy. A resume is also a sales tool.

I have to stop myself. My lips feel numb. I've had panic attacks in the past, but now they come more frequently. The writer in me observes and makes notes. I am no longer the same teacher who taught resumes; I am not the same person I was just six months ago. It's not the world around me that's changed, but me. I'm not sure what I'm going to do, how I'm going to approach this class at all. I keep telling myself that I'm all right, but I'm not. I'm performing. I'm trying to convince myself of my own pretense.

What I want to say to the students: Resumes are about conformity. They are oppressive tools to make everyone fit into the same box. It's just a resume, but it's far more dangerous than you know. Artists can't be made to fit in a box. They don't conform. And what I would tell the students is that if they really want to learn something from me today about resumes, something that they could hold and learn from in the future, it's that they should remain free for as long as they can. And if they really want to be artists, I would tell them, they had to turn the everyday-normal upside down and make others see differently. I'm rambling in front of the classroom. A nervous tremor shakes across the room. My thoughts overflow as I continue to discuss the purpose of a resume. I don't remember where I began, how to start, what I said.

Just a minute, I say.

I feel more anxiety coming on, more uncertainty about the future, about everything, and that's when I know that I have to sit down and drink water.

Next week, I say, bring your resume.

I dismiss the class.

Wobble

There are moments when I'm throwing a pot, when I'm concentrating so hard on raising that clay up into the air, using every muscle in my arms, the power of my wrists, the strength in my fingers and grip, when all that shattered energy inside me focuses briefly but intensely on one simple task. And during those brief moments, the body flies out of its shell, and I forget all my troubles, I forget my own name.

As I take the pot off the wheel, I feel a sense of accomplishment, but I also come back to the present moment, the reality surrounding me and the pot I've just thrown. Whether or not I succeed or fail on the wheel, throwing a pot is like taking a vacation from myself, and when I return, I can look at my life again, can see it fresh. Even though I am lost to the world, the studio feels like shelter, a place to wait for the storm to pass, for the clouds in my life to disperse.

I throw a lump of clay down on the wheel head. I wet my hands with water. The paradox of feeling both alive and dead imbues my life with a newfound freedom, a sense that the world is broken but wide open. I feel this way when I start to open the clay and bring it upwards. Anything is possible. I can make a vase or I can make a bowl.

When the wheel gets in motion, I feel my body press against the clay. When I pull the mud to the center of the wheel, I'm taking a measurement of not only the clay but also a measurement of myself: how much pressure to exert on the clay, how to let go of the clay. The hardest part about moving on in life without your partner is avoiding the past, dodging those old roads where you lived and breathed. It's hard to know when those moments will arrive because every object, every moment is a reminder. Like when driving, I keep glancing at the passenger seat expecting to see Julia. Each time reminds me.

One afternoon, I have a meeting with a student. Afterwards, I run into some colleagues, and we chat. I have to admit how good it feels to be part of the working world, to put oneself in the rhythm of teaching and learning. Our class meets, and I feel like a different teacher with them, but the class continues and then ends. See you next week, I say, but I really don't mean it. I'm just talking, just saying things. Instead of waiting for the elevator, I take the stairs. And as I'm descending, I'm thinking about how many flights I have to descend, and then imagining walking through the front doors, and in my mind I see an image of Julia waiting for me as she sometimes did when I got out of class. We'd walk home together or go get something to eat.

There are times when I'm throwing a pot and I'll feel the clay wobble like it is about to collapse on itself. It feels like all the work I've done is just about to be erased. What's important is that I've learned not to panic during these moments of wobbliness. Instead, I pretend that the pot is perfectly fine. I keep my body stiff and unmovable. My wrists turn into cement. I won't let anything push me off balance. I won't get distracted. I keep pulling a line upwards with the clay and capturing that feeling in my pots.

Walking

I am walking on one of my usual walks to tire myself out, to think, to escape, when I approach an empty field. It feels as if I've been walking for miles and miles, and my legs hurt, my feet are sore. I'm headed in the direction of a redwood barn resting on the horizon. It's a spring day, and the light feels weightless and warm on the exposed back of my neck. There is no hurry. There is no rush. I'm striding through tall grass towards a barn that feels familiar and quiet to me, although suddenly it occurs that I am lost, that I have no idea where I am, and that I have no recollection of this barn whatsoever. Two large oak trees lean and hover over me, their limbs like thick gnarled wrists, opening into a canopy of hands and fingers reaching down to earth. Gusts of wind bend the tips of grass. Beyond the barn, I see nothing but green landscape, meadows swaying on rolling hills, a languid emptiness that flows like many rivers.

In front of the barn, picnic tables are arranged underneath the shade of the oak. I'm walking towards these tables, drawn to them, wondering where everyone has gone, imagining a party in front of this barn, but the party is now elsewhere, the party is gone and the guests have dispersed. What remains on the tables is not party food but stacks of pots assembled for display, pots warm and fresh from a kiln—not my kiln, as I understand it, but someone else's kiln, the work of many others, all unknown to me. I see hundreds of pots spread across the space in front of the barn in what feels like endless stacks of bowls and platters, pots for as far as the eye can see.

In my escape, I lift pot after pot inside my hands, holding the fired clay to feel its weight, to judge its scale in relation to me. Who made these pots, I wonder? What can I learn from these bowls, plates, vases, cups, and mugs? Soft glazes. Dark glazes. I rub my hands on the inside curve, touch the unsanded bottom, my finger curling around the rim of the cup. There is no sound, just a warm spring light, a cool breeze, and the feeling that I have the rest of my life to look at these pots, to hold them, to understand them, to bring them into my life, to pick each one up and hold each one to the light.

Junkies

I meet Dana at hospice volunteer training. Part of the training involves role-playing, portraying either the grieving person or the hospice volunteer. We have learned some techniques about how to listen and create a supportive environment. Like me, Dana has lost her partner. Unlike me, she is over seventy, gray-haired, and walks with a cane. We are both the recipients of hospice grief support and have volunteered to be trained and to work in our communities.

Dana confesses to me she hopes to get an assignment to be a volunteer "watch." A "watch" is a volunteer who helps out a family as the individual dies at home. Usually, it's a matter of hours or days, but sometimes it's longer. Volunteers help families when they need a break. Dana says she hopes to be there when the person passes; she hopes to experience that moment because she missed her own husband's passing. I understand she isn't role-playing here, that she is serious, that there is something in it for Dana besides just helping other people. Perhaps I'm not any different.

After training, I volunteer in my community. I run a small grief support group, taking others through the same process that I am going through with grief. I am also assigned "cases" from the local hospice office. For one assignment, I am asked to help an elderly woman with her husband. She needs someone to sit with him while she drives to the drug store to pick up medication, to pick up groceries. Was I available?

These are the only people I want to be around, I think to myself. I am not like Dana; I don't want to see anyone die, but I desire to be around people in grief, people who tell the truth, people facing the impossible challenge of their lives. These are the people of my new community.

Chuck and Annie's small house sits in the middle of a retirement community, each cottage exactly like the other for the most part, all of them neatly landscaped, all of them quiet. When I first arrive, I see Chuck, who is in his eighties, very ill, sitting up in a medical bed in his living room which faces his back garden. I'm not a doctor, but I can feel death in the room. There are tubes to help him breathe, a drip to control his pain. I wash and scrub my hands in the kitchen sink. It is really important to be clean. Annie has taken over the dining room table with paperwork, prescriptions, monthly bills, folded laundry. She might be seventy years old herself, but she has incredible energy and she continues to fight valiantly alongside her husband.

"Birdy," she calls to him from the kitchen, "I'm going out for just a few minutes. This young man is going to sit with you. If you need anything, he will help you."

I sit with Chuck while he looks out the picture windows into his garden. I don't want Chuck to die while I am there; that isn't something I need to see. And yet, I realize he could die, and so I sit there wondering if I should talk or if I should be quiet. It's hard to say. Chuck can't speak, but he watches me closely. If I were Chuck, I would prefer the silence. I sit on the couch and draw pictures of teapots and coffee mugs in a notebook.

Annie returns, and I help her take down some boxes that she couldn't reach from shelves up high. She has me switch out their five-gallon water bottle on the water cooler. I give her my phone number if she needs to get information to me, but otherwise I tell her I will see her tomorrow, and she can plan her activities that way.

That evening, Annie leaves me a message that Chuck has passed and that she won't be needing me in the morning.

Some people are resilient in grief, while others disappear.

Love

When I finally asked Julia out on a date, I said, "Meet me at the Blue and Gold." She didn't see my invitation to meet on a date inside a bar as odd or unusual; she knew it was just my awkwardness, my utter lack of sophistication. We drank and played pool until we ended up back at her apartment where we stayed up all night drawing portraits of each other and talking about writers and magazines. Julia understood why I loved short stories and how much I burned with ambition to write beautiful ones.

At that moment, though, I was still single, living alone and paying rent for a storage space above a discounted stereo supplier on Fourteenth Street at Union Square. I was subletting the space from the artist, Stella Waitzkin, who lived at the Chelsea Hotel but who at one time used this space as a painting loft. We called it an "apartment," but only because it had a front door that locked. The space sat in the back of an abandoned storage area, tall windows facing the rooftops of the Village with beautiful southern light. There was no kitchen, no running water, no bathroom. I had a hot plate, a toaster, a coffee maker, and a small refrigerator. In the center of the room was a desk and word processor to write, a sleeping loft in the rear. There was an air conditioning unit in the window, and the light came from high windows that reached past the sleeping loft.

Another artist rented a space on the front side of the floor, but the building was empty and abandoned except for the street level that blasted pounding music all day long to lure customers inside for "discounted" boom boxes and stereo players. The floors were stripped, some walls destroyed, electrical wiring dripping from the ceilings, the copper pipes stolen. A few random lightbulbs illuminated the flight of stairs up from the clamor of Fourteenth Street. I was just one step away from a life as a squatter, but I didn't care because I had my own space to write, to think, and to read. At night, I heard footsteps of addicts traveling the hallways, but I'd never had any problems as most of them went to the roof and stayed there except in winter. There was an old restroom with dilapidated stalls and sinks where I could get water and use the toilet. I was living a feral life in the East Village, spending most of my time on the streets, writing in parks, going to see art, working temporary jobs, eating a diet of pizza and soda, and always carrying a towel in case I can shower at a friend's apartment.

Love came as a surprise in my life. I felt unprepared, so soon. Everything around Julia sparked with brilliance and drive. Late one winter weeknight, we walked together to a reading by Ismael Reed and his friends who were presenting their latest poems. The event took place inside an abandoned apartment building on Avenue C; an orange electric cord stretched from a van parked on the curb to several lamps inside to illuminate the path. We sat on folding chairs and wrapped our coats tightly around our bodies, watching the breath of each writer make halos while they read. This moment intoxicated, overwhelmed. Maybe it was the combination of living inside the world that constantly gurgled with art: on subway cars, on posters, murals, poetry written on the curbs, in cinema and galleries—all of it combined with falling in love with this beautiful woman who in so many ways was the opposite of me: short, opinionated, Jewish, completely open to the world, fearless. I was shocked to be with someone like Julia who loved art as much as me, was so knowledgeable, and whose hunger to explore was equal to my own.

After the reading, we wandered through the cold streets back to my space at Union Square. Walking up the stairs, I felt immune to the danger all around us. Being in love creates some type of shield that protects us. We fell into each other's arms inside my loft, and it was hours later when I woke up and saw snow, the roof covered with mounds of white. I felt Julia's breath on my back. Then I heard something on the roof. In the darkness, I saw two men outside as they disassembled the window, removed the air conditioner, and broke into my space.

A rush of cold air entered the room as they lifted the air conditioner and rested it on the roof. My body stiffened. Julia was curled behind me, still sleeping. What should I do? As I pondered that, the two men crawled inside my living space. I froze and tried not to move, not to get their attention. My thoughts ran quickly, and one thing I knew was that at that moment I would die to protect Julia. There was no doubt in my mind. I had never felt that way before about anyone or anything.

Before I could move, the two men walked through my space, their backs to me, unaware. Quickly, they undid the bolts on the front door and then sprinted into the hallway of the storage space, the light spilling through, footsteps echoing down the hall, and voices getting louder. I had a sinking feeling in my stomach that something bad was going to happen and I felt responsible for bringing Julia into this dangerous world when I saw another person on the roof, an outline of another figure, quickly squeezing in through the hole where the air conditioner once hung. He ran through the space and into the hallways, breathing heavily.

The police arrived later, and one of them helped me reattach the air conditioner. "What kind of idiot lives in a place like this?" asked the cop. He looked at Julia, "You married to this guy?" They assumed we were drug addicts, but we weren't. The walls were covered with Julia's paintings and drawings. The table was full of writing drafts and books. But what was there to say? Living in New York was dangerous in certain places, at certain times. And sometimes the cops were even scarier than the thieves. They took their flashlights and roamed the rest of the floor, but the addicts had fled.

Ash

Finally, it is time to fire the kiln.

Julia's kiln is called a "soda kiln." The pots she made before she died were intended to be fired in this kiln. A soda kiln is a type of kiln that creates an environment where the firing produces a certain atmosphere inside the kiln that leaves a mark on the pots by using soda ash and baking soda sprayed randomly inside the kiln near the end of the firing. I've been around and watched Julia fire this kiln, but it's advanced and really beyond a normal person's skill level.

Some potter-friends agree to join me and teach me how to fire Julia's work in the kiln. That is one thing I am learning from clay; you can't learn it alone. Information is passed on through trial and demonstration, the sharing of strategies. It is a Saturday morning, and the sky is clear and the grass has turned green from the heavy rains over the winter. A couple of cars are parked down the road, and I see Julia's friends carrying pots and food for everyone to eat. It feels good to have people here in the studio, firing the kiln. I know it would make Julia happy to see this studio working and once again firing kilns.

Everyone gathers at the studio, and we load the kiln; each person has brought along a pot or two to fire. I have made my first few pieces and placed them inside the kiln. I have a thousand questions for my friends about Julia's studio. What does it mean when a kiln is reduced? How close should the pots be stacked together? What if something happens and the stack collapses? My friend Joe Hawley sits with me and shows me how to use the pyrometer and gives me tips on how to make a cone pack. I'm discovering that there is a lot about pottery that has to do with a lot of stuff other than just throwing pots.

How can I describe the feeling in me of sitting next to a firing kiln eating barbeque chicken? Just the sound of the gas through the pipes and the idea of all those pots inside the kiln undergoing such change and transformation makes me relax. The fire burns all day and all evening. We eat food and sit at the picnic table talking about pots. I feel lucky to know these potters, to hear them talk about their own journeys in clay. I'm realizing that even though I'm not a potter and had never worked in clay, my life has been attached to clay ever since I met Julia, a relationship with clay that began by simply holding pots, eating out of one of her bowls, watching Julia make pots on the wheel.

It is late in the evening when the kiln reaches temperature. I follow everyone's lead and put on gloves and a mask. We divide up the tasks: someone starts to boil some hot water; another person prepares the soda ash and baking soda. We work together to prepare the kiln. My friend Joe takes me aside and asks me if I ever thought about putting some of Julia's ashes in the kiln.

I don't see why not. I return to our cabin and walk upstairs to the closet where sitting in a white paper bag is a box of Julia's ashes. I have not known what to do with Julia's ashes; when Joe mentions spraying some of them into the kiln, I immediately know it is a good idea.

We open the ports, and the inside of the kiln pulses with heat, deep orange in color, almost yellow. The temperature on the pyrometer reads 2200 degrees, flame shooting from the damper licking up into the night. The kiln bulges with heat and pressure. Just standing next to it, spraying soda into the interior, and I am covered in sweat. After half an hour the kiln glows and the pots are almost done.

Everyone gathers around the kiln. I have put a scoop of Julia's ashes into one of her bowls. Joe has figured out a way to use the shop vacuum to spray the ash inside the kiln. We practice one time to make sure it will work, and then I pour Julia's ashes into the tube of the dry vac. The flame lights up: orange, yellow, green, purple. There is an odor, the smell of human remains. After a few minutes, we close the damper on the kiln and turn off the gas. The firing is over.

When the kiln shuts off, everything becomes quiet.

Two days later, we gather again. The kiln has cooled. It is time to open up the door and see the pots. I pulled out a porcelain bowl that Julia had made. There are cups and vases, some small sculptures. My pieces come out of the kiln, one by one. There is joy in looking at these pots, seeing what my friends have made, analyzing how the fire affected each of them. I feel a weight has been lifted; Julia's work has been completed.

What happens a week later is what catches me most by surprise, and I feel a shifting in my world. I am sitting alone at my kitchen table, where I am eating soup out of my bowl that I have made, a bowl that has come from a kiln that was fired with Julia's ashes, pots coiled and pinched in her absence. It is a bowl that feels good to hold and is easy to use. I stop myself because it now occurs to me that I have never eaten out of a pot that I have made; I have always eaten out of the pots of others.

The world in my head is moving so fast that I have to stop and see what is happening. One moment I am making pots to help me think, to find a place to shelter, to try and comprehend the grief that consumes me. The next moment I am looking out over a whole new life, a different yet familiar world where perhaps I can survive. *Just make a cup. Just make a bowl.* But if I can make one bowl, if I can make one cup, I can make another bowl, and I can make another cup. The possibility exists that I can make a new life in clay.

This is what catches me by surprise that late afternoon in my kitchen, spooning soup from my handmade bowl, and for the first time since Julia's passing, dreaming and picturing of a space for me to live.

THE DRY STATE

Definition: The Dry State

A frenzied place of adolescence, rebellion, a pushing of the natural limits. The clay has been set, the form revealed, yet the work is not done; stickiness; the condition of not being easily persuaded; an area of quickening skills and risk-taking; the period in which an invisible impulse has been given a chance at life.

Doubt

Art consumes like a flame, always searching for oxygen, that burst of inspiration that can be transformed into the material, the beautiful, the sacred.

I've never felt so lost and bewildered. I was comforted the first time I tried to make a pot after Julia died even though some pots don't survive. I cling to the honesty of clay to speak to me the truth. Part of me intrinsically trusts pots without knowing why. That's the freedom of throwing pots: the getting lost in the clay, the stepping outside of myself and becoming adrift without being in any danger at all.

Starting out, I believe I am without talent. I am a writer, not an artist. I equate my own ignorance or not-knowing with being incompetent. But my mind is set on making a beautiful pot, so I keep trying and trying. I dream of making a big Korean Onggi pot. Other days I want to make a delicate tea set. My mind fills with images of pots and all the possibilities. I don't have any mechanical skills and have no idea how to make a pot, but I don't care about what I lack. What I have is an idea, a purpose—the dream to make a beautiful pot.

At the other side of the spectrum, there are others beginning in clay who cannot help but believe that everything they make is a work of genius. They almost can't keep this belief to themselves. They have to point out how great they are to everyone else even though they don't know anything. I don't understand these types of people. In a way, I envy those persons who believe they have hidden, secret talents.

Maybe the hardest thing about starting in clay is letting go of yourself and your own story you tell yourself. The strange thing about my experience is although I am determined to make a beautiful pot, I don't overcome my fears and doubts by trying. To this day, I haven't conquered this idea that I'm not talented. The lack of belief continues, yet I won't be stopped. For me, every moment of my new life feels that way; I can't overcome those doubts and fears, but I can learn to live alongside them and do what I need to do. I don't need to give up.

Profile

Pots don't like to be alone; they prefer to be members of a herd. At the same time, pots are introverts with extroverted tendencies. Think of pots in terms of packs. See them together as a gesture found in nature. A table filled with handmade pots sways like fields of waving corn, undulating and alive. The soup bowl and the salad plate don't match, but watch how they connect together on the kitchen table, how they communicate like plants spreading their roots through fingertips and touch.

Awake

In my twenties, I spent afternoons at the McDonald's on 1st Avenue in the East Village. The interior was one floor beneath street level, a cemented bunker both filthy and dangerous; greasy tables, overflowing garbage bins, addicts sleeping, strangers shivering. I was addicted to soda drinks and would drink cup after cup. I came there to write and to think and to observe. Each day possessed a powerful dynamic, discovering how to survive in New York without any money, a degree in English literature, and no useful skills. All I knew was that I wanted to be a writer.

And here I am now, decades later, standing in line at an interstate highway rest stop outside Sacramento, already high from the stench of chemical fat and gasoline fumes. It's raining, and I have pulled over to let the storm pass when a feeling of serenity washes over me. This is my first time in a fast-food franchise in over twenty years, and I am making the most of it. I have ordered a massive amount of junk hamburgers and French fries and onion rings. When my number is called, I carry a plastic tray of heated meat patties and grease to an empty plastic booth to once again sit down to recklessly pollute my body and soul.

I am not alone in saying that the dining rooms of McDonald's offer some consolation in life. The rest stop gasoline and packaged buffet feels like the right place for me, neither beginning nor end, but somewhere in between. My brain floods with food chemicals; the thoughts turn to pots. Vases, bowls, jars. I soothe myself with imagined pots I might someday make when my skills get better. I feel like I've forgotten what I know about writing, as if all that knowledge perished. Every day, I see the walls around me burning, memories disappearing, a life moving away. And yet there is an energy when I think about pots. There is a constant rush. Desperation generates boldness. My mind searches for places to attach, streams of life, separate tracks moving in different directions.

I finish my meal and merge back onto the interstate in one seamless gesture. I am about three hours from home. The rain has stopped. It's not just that I'm alone, but also that I'm entering an unknown world with no concept of itself, no idea where it is headed, a sensation that reminds me of that period in my youth between leaving home and going out in the world to become a writer.

Gravity

It's always a pleasant surprise to pick up a mug and feel its lightness. We don't expect objects we use to be light. On a subconscious level, we prepare ourselves for weight out of habit, as a means of self-defense. I brace myself in the smallest and largest ways for the heaviness of the world. Gravity and how we accommodate gravity's expression shapes our lives. So when the cup isn't heavy, when it seems to fly through the air defying expectations, I feel a lightness in my own self, and I am charmed by this cup and its ability to surprise and engage.

Kiln Building

I walk with friends on an empty country road that circles the site where we are constructing a legacy kiln in honor of Julia. Our day of work is over. A gray light filters overhead, and the air dampens beneath the arbor of trees, though I sense spring approaching. More than ever, I am sensitive to the movements of the sun, the passage of time. Every day remains a challenge to absorb the loss.

I am in North Carolina to build a kiln in Julia's honor as I navigate a world absent her love and understanding. Grief is new to me, like these kilns that rest outside the clay studios of Penland. I am ignorant because I'm not a potter, not a builder. I've never lost someone I loved. I'm forty-seven years old and a widower: no children, no family. At the moment, I have no job.

I'm learning how to build a kiln with the guidance of the kiln designer and artist Mark Peters, a friend and mentor of Julia's. We are walking on the road that encircles the campus of Penland School of Craft in the foothills northeast of Asheville, a place where Julia studied and worked as a teaching assistant in ceramics. I can't think of a more moving tribute to Julia than making an instrument to create art here at Penland. Her friends Paul, Nora, Katie, Denise, and Julia's cousin Anna are part of the crew erecting the kiln in Julia's honor. We walk as a group down the center of the two-lane road. It is late afternoon, and we have labored all day stacking brick, cutting brick, mixing mortar. Tomorrow, we will begin work on the chimney. Despite the fact we have not completed the kiln, this late afternoon walk brings a feeling of accomplishment.

We enjoy the moment because we are done with the day and because manual labor can help ease psychic pain. I am fighting another flu virus, however, a fact I don't share with anyone because I sense they worry about me too much already. I am overweight and taking too many pills to help me sleep and aid me in staying calm. I have resumed smoking nicotine after years of not smoking. I am drinking too much and drinking alone. My body is breaking down from prolonged grief, and though I'm able to function and navigate, within me lives a pent-up rage.

We head in the direction of the ceramic studio of Cynthia Bringle, a Penland potter and educator who was a mentor and teacher to Julia and her friends, to share a glass of wine and meet up with some local potters. We'll toast to Julia and her memory, and I will dodge hidden potholes threatening to surface. I know by now that grief swells and overtakes me when I least expect it.

The Penland road circles a series of knolls and empty pastures that fold like wide swaths of green drapery. In the background, hanging like a scrim across the horizon, the Blue Ridge Mountains. Despite the circumstances, the mountains of North Carolina draw me to them, to a place deep in the woods where two years ago I spent eight weeks writing a fiction manuscript. There are ghosts everywhere I look inside this beautiful part of the world, and the strange part is that I am one of those ghosts, an old me, a version of me no longer present on this earth. I recall walking onto these pastures two years ago in the middle of the night and lying on the cut grass with Julia as we both gazed at the lights of Penland, silhouetted artists working in their studios, the stars overhead.

I have been told by many people that I am on a journey of grief, and these friends of Julia's are grieving as well. Coming together is a way of forging solidarity against the absurd idea that Julia is no longer among us. Building a kiln is a way to help each other survive. I understand our purpose. I wear a brave face and agree with these ideas in theory, but on the inside, I'm separate. I'm wandering around by myself, invisible to the world, still wondering what the hell happened to Julia, to me, to us.

Llama

"Has anyone seen the llamas?" asks Paul.

Whenever I think of Penland School of Craft, I see an image in my mind of the two llamas walking along the fence railing in front of the campus. The pair roam the pastures and hillsides of Penland, two shaggy animals whose awkward gait would be endearing if they weren't sometimes so aggressive. I saw them on one occasion from the parking lot, and they came up to me expecting to be fed. Spotting the llamas is part of the Penland experience, but so far no sightings.

Nora and Denise shake their heads. Our friend, Katie, might have seen the llamas. She's taken her car down to the studio, but she knows the stories of the Penland community.

"Maybe they go to Florida in the winter," I joke.

I am being that courageous widower who can somehow manage to grieve and make jokes at the same time. I don't recognize this person I'm becoming. Sometimes I think it's up to me to put others at ease, to make our grief less stressful. Random indescribable worry hovers nearby, bits and pieces of me streaming all around but never coming together. We circle a horseshoe-shaped field looking out over the pastures, thinned foliage of trees, vines pushing upwards about to bud. Still no sign of the llamas.

"Wherever the llamas are, they're sitting next to a heater," jokes Nora. Though it's cold to work outside, I am having an opportunity to get to know Paul, Nora, and Denise, different from when I was Julia's husband. The three of them have their own families, partners, jobs, businesses. They live in Florida, Massachusetts, New York. They have taken time out of their lives to join Mark Peters and me to build this kiln. Grief recalibrates everything, including relationships.

Mark Peters is a local. He lives up on Roan Mountain. The area around Penland is populated by craftspeople and artists, potters and painters, woodworkers and glass artists. To me, Mark is a quintessential studio potter living up in the mountains, making his own pots, and following his own vision. Julia had been one of Mark's students and worked as his assistant building a kiln. We ask Mark: Have you seen the llamas?

"That's a sad story," he says in his light Tennessee drawl. "I don't know if it's true, but nobody had seen the llamas for months until the story came out."

None of us has heard anything. We are visitors to this place. We are here to be part of the Penland universe of arts and crafts, where handmade art is the local religion. Stepping into the world around Penland is like entering a dream where there are no chain stores, no television, no advertising. It's a place for making, for working with your hands. We are desperate for real stories, to drink in this utopian world of craft and mountain legends.

Mark tells us that the llamas must have been walking at night, not here near the campus of Penland but further south. The animals were always together and never apart. They were owned by a farmer who had gotten old and become a recluse. He fed the llamas, but he let them roam inside his neighbor's farm that hadn't been used for over a decade. He probably shouldn't have allowed his animals to go on his neighbor's land. It wasn't legal, but the neighbor didn't ever object because he didn't live there; he lived in Asheville. The llamas would wander up the neighbor's land toward the Penland campus for food and water, then back to the farm where they lived with the farmer's two dogs and four chickens.

About a year ago, the neighbor who owned the nearby land sold his property to someone from Charlotte who wanted to build a second home. Mark pointed to an area where the house would be built. The first thing the new owner needed to do was to dig a well. A group of laborers drilled and dug one hundred feet into the earth, neglecting to protect the area around the mouth of the well. And instead of digging at an angle, they dug straight down at ninety degrees. What happened will always be a mystery. The llamas must have been out at dusk; maybe the light had failed, or maybe they simply were distracted, but one of the llamas fell into the well, broke its neck, and eventually died.

Well

The size of the well depends on the impact on your life. The deeper the grief, the deeper the well. There are all kinds of grief that range from the mundane to the profound, moments of discreet regret or times of staggering loss. At some point, however, you don't see it coming. The earth opens up beneath your feet, and the lights go dark.

It's doubly intense to go through trauma and simultaneously observe how the brain changes, thought patterns warping under different pressures. My background as a writer teaches me to witness everything and to take notes. Out of reflex, I'm watching myself, perceiving how my brain latches on to certain thoughts and images. When I close my eyes, everything is dark at first, but then I see the llamas. I'm decoding this new world, searching for signals that will help me endure.

Nora asks, "What happened to the other llama? The one that survived?"

Mark explains that llamas need a herd; they can't live alone. He didn't know what happened to the other llama, but he assumed since the farmer was old that he sold the other llama or if that wasn't possible, he'd killed it to put it out of its misery.

It's the mark of a lost soul who doesn't even know he's

already lost. Perhaps it's the cumulative effects of trauma, as the numbing walls of self-protection clear themselves over days, weeks, months, when I become able to view a larger context. Every story, even if it's a bad story, contains within it a conclusion, a sum of its own equation, but not stories about grief. Stories about grief are open-ended. For example, none of us will ever know what happened to the other llama, the one that lived, where he went or how he managed to survive.

Blame

Are you writing?

No, I am not writing. I have to be honest that I have no interest in writing. I have no interest in reading. My brain is overworked trying to understand what happened to Julia, where she went, and the pain and suffering she endured at the end of her life. I don't have space in my brain to read and write, but many people ask me this question. These questions surprise me, catch me off-guard. But these questions are hopeful, I eventually understand. My friends are pulling me back to the normal world where I wrote and read as passion, and they believe writing will help me heal.

This is an issue I'm thinking about as I sit in Cynthia Bringle's studio at Penland listening to everyone talk. Julia's cousin, Anna, took a bus from Savannah, Georgia to be here. She is a young art student. Her talent reminds me of Julia. There is a lot of laughter in the studio, a lot of looking at pots. I hear someone telling the story of the llama, and they mention wondering how long the llama lay in the well before he eventually died, and how they buried the llama inside the well because the animal was too heavy to retrieve. I'm numb, moving in a type of emotional slurry, buoyed and yet fatigued.

"Are you writing?"

No, I am not writing, and now when I think about writing, I get angry at myself. Just right here in Cynthia's studio, a terrible wave of guilt descends upon me. An overarching regret emerges for all the time I lost with Julia because I required time alone to write. I'm seeing my actions as selfish even though I know they are not selfish because Julia and I gave each other the necessary room to do our own art. But I was the one who required time alone. I know this as fact, yet I'm blaming myself, feeling angry and confused and heartbroken that I can't change the past.

Are you writing?

No, I'm not writing, and I don't believe that I will ever write again because I'm transferring my anger to books and literature, and all the time spent reading them, all the days spent believing in them. Literature let me down because books made me imagine life had some sort of composition, some organizing principle that framed the world. All of it was wrong, the ideas beautiful but empty. Julia is dead, and there is no reason that books can show me that will help me understand.

Are you writing?

No, I'm not writing because when I look at my writing all I see is failure and wasted time. This is how I see things now: in terms of time. All the time spent writing, trying to write, rewriting, sending work out, rejections, revising, sending work out, rejections, rejections, rejections. And yet I kept writing, and now I'm angry at myself for ignoring the truth and not accepting failure.

Are you working on something?

No, I'm not, but today I was carrying many bricks back and forth and moving lots of heavy objects and working alongside some wonderful people and at the end of the day it looked like we might have built something real and permanent called a kiln.

So, no, I'm not writing.

Home

I'm surprised by how much I'm learning when I'm not writing. I lie awake at four in the morning in a room at Penland unable to go back to sleep. The air feels charged. I'm in a state of sustained alarm. I don't confess this to other people, but I still sense that even in a deathly realm, Julia is in pain and searching for me. This is how my brain absorbs. My life feels both simultaneously carpet-bombed and yet explosive; all around me is ruin and failure, but also bursting on the periphery is a new awakening, a new identity. I am exhausted but wide awake. In a few hours, I'm leaving to return home.

I get up and get dressed to take a farewell walk along a network of trails behind Penland as the sun starts to appear in the sky. Whenever I leave a place these days, I say goodbye to it. Today, I am headed to the Asheville airport to fly back to California. Later this evening, I will drive two hours north of San Francisco and return home to our cabin, and the cabin will be empty. The hits will continue to keep coming. However, I also notice something else: I am thinking about how much freedom grief gives me, how many of my previous concerns are no longer concerns, and it feels good to be rid of them. Strangely, I'm finding the positives in grief; for example, I am no longer shy. I no longer care and have the energy to be shy. There isn't enough time left to be shy, and so, thankfully, that is no longer a concern.

Studio Junkie

I bring with me the discipline of a writer to the learning of throwing pots. I busy myself by working in the studio, living inside a new world that requires my body and my hands, my strength, my coordination, my physical ability. My body aches at the end of the day, but my mind feels lighter.

When the clay gets in motion on the wheel, and I feel my body pressing the mound of mud to center it on the wheel, I'm making an estimation of myself, about how much pressure to exert on the clay. I'm also learning how to make my own path in this studio, how to impress myself in Julia's artistic space. I understand the larger questions, but I'm impatient. I want to get there now. It's similar to grief; I want the pain of grief to be over. I want to feel better now, but I know it's going to take time.

When I finally get the clay centered, I begin to lift the clay with my fingers, and there are times when I feel the clay wobble. Suddenly, my hands and my head feel miles apart, and the clay collapses. It would be too easy to blame the clay and walk away. The truth is that sometimes I get lost on the wheel, begin to doubt myself, and the whole thing goes south.

I will not admit it because I am still angry at literature and writing, but it is true that being a writer has prepared me for learning how to throw pots in ways I never imagined. I can think of these disasters in clay as trashed drafts of beginnings, explorations, stories that end up nowhere. Failure is central to the act of writing, so perhaps disaster doesn't shock me like it might others. I start over again.

And if I just mentally step back, if I look at my life in terms of pots, I can almost see it because my life is contained within this studio and all these pots that surround me. I notice myself finding ways in Julia's studio despite all the empty chaos around me. I'm thinking if I could bottle this uncertainty in her studio, that instinct in me with clay that doesn't seek an equilibrium, if I could simply take that instinct and apply it to the rest of my life to become comfortable feeling imbalanced and lost, I might someday find my way through this grief.

That's what I'm thinking while I throw cups on the wheel, but in the meantime I understand that I have to make a lot of pots in order to make one good pot. It's not something I can impose because of my will. Pots rise off the wheel head when they are ready. And there are certain days when I feel something inside me leap forward in my craft, a smoothness where there was a previous chaos, more clay lifting off the wheel and becoming lighter. A path opens up between my brain and my hands that previously did not exist, and suddenly I am pulling a handle on a cup to create a mug, and the handle is half decent, not pitiful.

But there are studio days when I am so tired, not just from working with clay, but with everything, and it reminds me of the kind of tired I felt trying to speak Spanish at a party where no one spoke English, my brain doing double-time trying to extract words to express myself in a foreign language. In the same way, I'm living two lives in two languages: the expression of clay and the discovery of making pots, and at the same time, the other world, a parallel track that Julia and I would see together, the universe of the experiences that escaped us. Concentrating so hard creates its own fatigue.

This evening, I am trimming a big bowl, probably the biggest bowl that I've ever made, and it weighs too much. I have to trim this bowl down to a reasonable weight and into a beautiful shape. Julia has a whole box of trimming tools, and I take them out one by one and run the blades over the surface, creating a shape in my mind's eye, the curve of the outside of the bowl, carving away at the clay with my tools. By the end of the evening, a few pounds of clay are trimmed and lie in shreds at the bottom of my feet.

Plastic

It will take me several years to understand the obvious: that the bag wrapped in plastic I open to retrieve clay to make pots has been taken directly from the earth, mixed and processed for throwing, inserted and packaged in plastic and then placed inside a cardboard box where it sat on truck until delivery to my ceramic supply store. Maybe it's the plastic wrapping that creates the disconnect, the inability to draw the line from the source. Like bottled water. Or remembering that a can of tuna fish buried in the back of your kitchen cabinet once upon a time swam in the turquoise depths of the ocean. Maybe the freest moment of each day begins with me pulling a chunk of clay from its bag and letting my hands figure out what they want to make.

Haircut

I am sitting in a chair getting my hair cut when I feel the palm of her hand on the back of my neck. The young woman cutting my hair uses a razor. And after she is done, her hand rubs the back of my neck, a tender massage. It is healing and unconscious and innocent, and then it is over. Minutes later, she hands me a mirror to show me how the back of my head looks with my new cut. I don't really care how I look, but she is proud of her work, and I understand. I give her a tip and walk out the door into the parking lot, realizing that I haven't been touched by a woman in over a year.

Physique

The Feet

My hands feel clumsy, and then at a certain point, gain a fluency I never knew I had. There are ways to hold tools, to use leverage, to soften my impatience, to solve problems that only require some experience and some faith in myself and my own skills. I discover that my hands possess their own cleverness, their own ways of supporting my intentions with a pot, imparting information, and figuring out ways to persuade the clay into unlikely forms.

The Legs

The world contains motion; I no longer statically sit in a chair and read or write. I am up all day long, moving, moving, moving. Sitting down and thinking becomes a dangerous preoccupation, so I work in the studio. I abandon my writing journals. There is always work in the clay studio; the sink trap needs to be replaced; the burners on the kiln need to be cleaned; buckets of clay that require recycling. The list is endless.

The Waist

I have never learned a craft with my hands, but I am watching videos and looking in books about how to make pots, how to throw light pots, how to trim a bowl, how to engineer a form that can be used for the function of pouring, sipping, holding, containing, showcasing food or flowers. But craft is not so much about research as about doing, training your mind to think with your hands.

The Chest

My attention span barely exists anymore, but the clay forces me to concentrate, to think over and over again. The rhythm of constant failure, the doomed outlook for most of my pots, allows me a freedom from myself. Today I want to make an oval pot, so I must throw the pot without a bottom, raise the clay without a foundation, and then form it into an oval shape. But my hands won't cooperate. My balance is way off. The pot collapses. I try again.

The Neck

Grief has made my body a stranger to me from neglect and indifference. Now as I start working with clay, picking up twenty-five-pound bags of clay, throwing twenty-five pounds of clay, carrying around twenty-five pounds of clay, boxing twenty-five pounds of clay, my body awakens. All day long, there is labor. There is no sitting down. I stand while I work.

The Mouth

I am accustomed to nervous exhaustion from teaching and writing, a type of exhaustion that becomes physical when the nervous system breaks down. My head throbs and my back is sore, but my body isn't in pain.

Throwing pots all day is different. At night, my body aches so bad that I start dropping tools and making stupid mistakes. Tiring myself out physically plays catch-up with my mental and emotional fatigue. The synapses in my brain are firing simultaneously like bombs exploding, but at least there is hope that at the end of the day, I will be able to sleep out of pure physical exhaustion.

Form

My friends invite me to a party in Oakland. It's time, they say. Who am I to argue? I don't know what is good or bad. I say, yes, I will go to the party, even though this sounds like a horrible idea, something I would never choose. But I'm going with all the wrong choices now. This is the world of bewilderment and grief.

It is a warm evening. I'm sweating just sitting in the driver's seat, looking for the address of the apartment building. I don't know Oakland at all; I have no sense of direction here. Immediately, I regret my decision to go to this party, but I park my car near Lake Merritt and study the numbers on the mailboxes. The apartment building is built into a steep hill, a curving path of steps against an ivy-covered staircase, music and voices filtering through the leaves of Eucalyptus.

One obstacle is I am supposed to meet my friends inside the party, but I don't know the host. Why did I agree to this? I look up and see colored lights and silhouettes of bodies leaning over the deck of the apartment. I think for a moment: I can't do this. I can't walk into a room full of people I don't know, people who want to get together and have a good time. It's not their fault. There isn't room in me for letting go, laughing, dancing, being non-serious. I stall and walk around the neighborhood. I smoke a cigarette. I think to myself: this is ridiculous. I've come all this way to Oakland; I should just go inside.

I convince myself to walk into the party, me and my estranged grief, into a room full of people I don't know, people who don't know about me. For an evening I will pretend, and I am going to act just like them, like everyone else. I'm going to see if I can do this, if I can blend and be like others. My two friends, the couple who invited me to meet them at the party, see me at the door and come to greet me. They introduce me to the host. I have done it. I have gotten through the front door. Meanwhile, I eat crackers, drink wine and talk to my friends. They introduce me to others. I appear to be having fun; I believe no one would ever know how broken I feel inside. The inside of the apartment fills with more people.

The more crowded it gets, the more I drink. I am hot and getting sweaty, and I am outside this group of people; I am not among them even though I am standing in a crowded kitchen listening to people tell stories and make jokes. It's taking a lot of energy to pretend to enjoy myself. If pretending were only for one night, I would not have a problem. My real fear is that this sensation is not temporary, that feeling separated and alone is my permanent state.

The music gets louder, and people begin to dance. I keep drinking and then move out of the apartment to the back stairs. Sweat continues to pour down my back and soak my shirt. The thought crosses my mind that I am having a heart attack because my chest tightens and I am finding it difficult to breathe. I am walking down the front concrete steps, breathing heavily, then panting. My friends see me leaving and run to catch up with me. As I explain how hot I had become inside the party and how I am finding it hard to breathe, I start to feel better. It is cooler outside. I feel a breeze coming off the bay. My breathing becomes regular again, the muscles in my chest relax. My friends sit me down on the curb by my car. It takes a few minutes for me to realize what my friends already know: I am having another panic attack.

Disaster

I feel alive inside the clay studio. Even from the early days, I never see clay as a hobby; I never perceive clay as a therapy. In the early days of making pots, the only thing I can think about is how to make a beautiful pot, and that is where all of my energies turn.

I'm learning skills, but I'm also understanding what makes a beautiful pot, at least to me. As my techniques sharpen, so does my perspective on how to look at a pot. And the only way to really know my own taste is to make a lot of pots, to push harder, to see them come alive on the pottery table and feel the excitement or disappointment. I'm anxious to see what I can do, what's possible.

I don't feel discouraged despite all the disaster of these early pots, these hasty attempts to try and make something sophisticated. I'm not just thinking about making work on the wheel, but I'm beginning to anticipate how I want the pots to look when they emerge from the kiln.

Recipes

Nothing is ever what it first appears. Throwing pots is not simply working on the wheel; it's also about making other stuff on the periphery such as mixing glazes and firing kilns and trying to understand all three different processes at once. I don't have any idea what a glaze is and why glazes are needed other than glazing seems like something most potters do. I'm so over my head in terms of what I'm trying to accomplish, but I know enough to understand that I have to research. I have to learn.

Malcolm's Shino

Nepheline Syenite 40

F-4 Feldspar 13

Kaolin 18

Ball Clay 9

Soda Ash 17

Glazes can be clear or opaque. They can exhibit a satin-type surface, a gloss, or a matte. Most glazes bring a light to a pot because the glaze reflects luminance more significantly than clay. But maybe more importantly, the glaze brings the clay to a level where a bond has been created, something unique between the clay body and the glaze itself. And it's that bond that's difficult at times to make because the ingredients might be off, or the temperature might have cooled too fast, or because the clay body and the glaze simply don't get along.

Willie Helix

Nepheline Syenite 42

Whiting 20

Silica 25

Kaolin 12

Copper Carbonate 5

Bentonite 2

What I learn to like about glazes is that they reflect more clearly the transformation of the clay itself. When clay gets fired, the color changes by becoming darker or lighter, and the clay becomes harder and more solid; but a person on the outside has no idea what the clay has undergone to arrive at this hardened state. The clay doesn't reveal much. Glazes, on the other hand, especially in atmospheric kilns, can communicate the heat and transformation that is experienced in a kiln in a way that bare clay can't.

Val's Taffy

Cornwall Stone 46

Whiting 34

Kaolin 20

Red Iron Oxide 4
Titanium Dioxide 6

It takes weeks to decipher recipes, to understand the basic vocabulary of what these numbers and names mean, how to measure these ingredients using a scale, how to mix the glazes to the right ratio of water. I discover bags of raw materials that match the names of the ingredients: Nepheline Syenite, Custer Feldspar, Cornwall Stone. I determine the numbers next to the names of the ingredients to be the percentage or the number of grams to create the glaze. On certain days, it feels like I'm trying to decipher a hidden code, that underneath these numbers, beneath the chemistry of a glaze lies something not necessarily profound but otherwise complete.

Dolly's Russian Hotel

Nepheline Syenite 8
F-4 Feldspar 54
Spodumene 19
Kaolin 7
Barnard Slip 8
Soda Ash 5

There's a lost story behind every glaze recipe, the forgotten story of the person or inventor, a potter who measured and tested clay materials to create something unique. The glaze is often named after its creator, but in a casual, ceramic way like

"Cathy's Blue Celadon" or "Tim's Toasty Red." The story of Cathy and how she came to make a celadon that was so beautiful she shared it with the world has been forgotten, but this very difficult-to-achieve powder-blue celadon can be recreated if you follow these ingredients.

There is a wealth of human endeavor that possesses a private ambition, something that drives some of us to explore avenues of interest with the fervor of a person of faith, someone who believes that deep in the hole of investigation, somewhere between a few grams of soda ash or substituting Red Art clay, a truth resides, a beautiful shade of powder blue or a dripping rivulet of fake wood ash.

Woo Blue

G-200 Feldspar 4158
Whiting 1784
Silica 2675
Ball Clay 1283
Bentonite 100
Red Iron Oxide 391
Rutile 391

One basic misconception put to rest early: Glazing a pot is not like painting. It's not like painting a room, or painting a piece of furniture, or painting on canvas. That's what's so confusing at first. Glazes are made of raw materials mixed with water. The color of the liquid glaze applied to the pot is completely indifferent to the color the glaze becomes when heated to a high temperature and turned into glass. We are conditioned to believe that what we see is the truth, especially with something like color, especially color coming off your paintbrush. You have to quiet the voice in your head that says to put some gray liquid over there when the gray liquid will transform during the firing into the color brown.

Julia's Pale Green Speckle

Neph. Sye. 37.23

Silica 35.10

Dolomite 10.63

Whiting 8.51

Barium Carbonate 6.38

EPK China Clay 2.12

In that way, glazing is a type of imagination, a method of thinking about a time in the future when these raw materials will melt and vitrify with the clay to create a glassy surface filled with color. It's a bit like dreaming about something in your head and then drawing it on paper, but almost in reverse. And I keep thinking that beneath all these numbers and calculations is the idea that glazing is a type of approximation, a general willing of an idea into the chaos and atmosphere of a kiln and letting go a little bit. And it's the letting go that's important to me, to understand that everything in the future is an approximation.

Space

The inside of an empty bowl is one of the most peaceful places in the world. When I look inside a bowl, I don't know exactly what I'm looking for or why I'm looking; I feel the pull of the space and I want to experience the curve more closely. The interior of a bowl or a poem is a type of dream galaxy, a crossing of the invisible world with the visible world, and perhaps that is why when faced with a jar, I must reach for the knob to lift the lid to look inside. I absolutely must.

Blindness

My father, when he was alive, was an outwardly friendly man, but he had a horrible temper. When he was angry, his face blushed a deep pink color and he would yell until he expelled all his pent-up frustrations with his life. Yelling came naturally to him. He hated his job and tolerated his family sort of like a second job. I think he loved us, but I don't know.

My father had a workbench in the garage where he supposedly repaired broken vacuums or a flat tire on one of our bikes. Whenever my parents purchased something which required assembly, the situation devolved into cursing and swearing. My father had no patience. Though he considered himself an athlete, he didn't like physical work. He preferred to sit in his chair and watch sports—a sports addict. He would yell at the television screen, pacing around nervously during overtimes and tiebreakers.

One day as a child, I tagged along with him working in the backyard. He handed me a rake and said, "Don't kill yourself." A half hour later, I tripped on the blade and cut my chin on the cement, blood gushing into the pile of raked leaves. He yelled at me for tripping and bending the rake. It was only when my mother returned home from errands that I went to the hospital and received four stitches across my lips. After a while, I stay away from my dad and tools altogether.

In high school, I got the idea to get far away from home by going to college. I did not inform my parents that I wanted to be a writer, not an accountant. My mother confided to me, "Vince, our only dream for you is that one day you'll work in a tall office building with your own office, your own desk, and your own phone line." For my parents, children of the Great Depression, the professional world looked like a safer bet than the world of blue-collar workers.

So I grew up not knowing how to use tools. I didn't come from an environment where we constructed things or tried to understand how things worked. I survived into adulthood without knowing how to change a tire. I have a toolbox but I avoid using tools because I don't know how to use them. I feel a huge gap in me, a place where I am vulnerable because of this handicap. It is sort of like going around blind to the world, missing a huge component of the experience of living— figuring out the material of your life and engaging your mind and your hands.

Brooklyn

Yes, I was the young married guy looking up with the straw face and squinted eyes, exchanging glances with you as I struggled up the subway steps, wearing a wrinkled dress shirt, a loose tie, khaki pants, black tennis shoes, a gray winter parka with a backpack thrown over my shoulder hauling student papers and textbooks on rhetorical strategies from borough to borough, county to county, state to state. I was the guy sitting across from you on the subway car, pale as paper, living on bagels and cream cheese, staring at nothing, swollen glands, a plastic container of last night's leftovers poking from my satchel. Imagine the empty sound of shuddering trains as they crossed railroad ties outside of Newark. Now what was I thinking? What lingered in my brain on those underground rides beneath the East River? I try to recall those moments during my commuter campaigns to faraway New Jersey or comatose Long Island, but I feel as if I've lost those moments, that I can never recapture that time sitting on subways numb to myself. I recall flags waving in front of a nondescript government building where I walked up the front steps, made copies inside the instructor's lounge, and then proceeded to teach writing and critical thinking to freshmen and sophomores. You might imagine that something

I assigned and discussed with these classes, readings from great writers and great thinkers, would have sparked a flame, but that is not the case. Every destination to a new school was a new job, a different set of angry faces who didn't understand why they had to take a writing course. It was up to me to provide reason and motive, to demonstrate the necessity of writing in order for them to learn. That was the premise of my life, my blindness to the beauty I viewed as obstacles, the same struggles, the same routines, the chaotic sameness that happens to all those who live in New York for too many years. As rich as the experience had been of teaching people how to write, I wasn't immune to the constant pounding of the cement, the unforgiving pavement, the fluorescent lights, the feeling of factory-like thinking, the daily intensity that eventually transforms itself, in a certain manner of speaking, unfortunately, into an anonymous grind.

The luster of New York waned. I felt frustrated living in close proximity to so much art and writing but without the time or space to create any of my own because I was too busy working to stay afloat. We bought a used car and decided to leave New York, to get on the road, to drive to California, to build a new life because we could, because we were free with the liberty of having nothing to lose.

Music

At night I go to bed and close my eyes, and all I can see is the wheel turning around and around. When I'm walking, I'm thinking about pots and replaying how I made a certain shape and how I could make it less heavy, be more concentrated when I throw, limit my movements and be clear. Or I wonder what a pot might look like if one drew its chemical composition as musical notation. I see kaolin possessing a high-pitched vibration, a tenor-like clarity. The stoneware bringing the bass, and terracotta the rhythm, the heart.

A frog in my backyard finds its way into the bottom of a discarded porcelain bowl and cannot crawl its way out, its webbed toes slipping against the interior glaze. The frog croaks and croaks, its throaty bellow amplified by the concaved hollow of the bowl. All day long the cries are broadcast until I can bear it no longer. I lift the frog in the palm of my hand toward the lip of the bowl. He hops from my fingers to save his life and discovers his freedom in the shade of a rock. The frog moves on eventually, but the pot retains the residue of grief, a melody that lingers in my mind as I avoid its gaze whenever I pass.

Estrangement

I have always been a reader, and so it is unusual not to carry a book around with me in my backpack or have a book by my bedside. Books are companions, ongoing conversations, explorations of different worlds, but I fear wasting time on books that aren't truthful. I realize how impossible it is to concentrate, to take myself away from my ruined world and enter the imagination of reading.

However, I want to make beautiful pots, and eventually I discover Julia's library of books on ceramics. I am ravenous for information, eager to understand what seems so daunting, so overwhelming. At first, I look at pictures of pots, but then I start to read and become more curious. I discover *Pioneer Pottery* by Michael Cardew, an English potter from the mid-20th century. In the preface, he writes, "This book is intended for those individuals who want to strike out on their own and make their own pottery."

I sit down to read for the first time in a year. I switch on my reading lamp. The page bounces with white, but it's the words that pop out to me, the voice behind the language. I am reminded of the thrill that occurs when a voice lifts from the page, the moment of recognition when the tone and the language sound so intimate and assured that the story seems inevitable. Cardew writes, "But as the work went on, I realized that pioneering is not a matter of geography but of the heart."

From descriptions describing digging your own clay and processing it to throwing pots on your own self-built wheel inside your own self-designed and constructed clay studio, there is no topic in pottery that isn't covered in *Pioneer Pottery*. The explanations of correct forms and methods feel like dictums. The opinions are strong, never wavering. Questions are answered before they are even posed. There are lengthy descriptions of quartz inversion and thermal expansion that are readable. Does he have an opinion on the applied arts? Yes, Cardew has an opinion. Cardew writes so well and so comprehensively, the type of writing that is both macro and micro simultaneously, no detail too specific, no philosophical subtext too wide for his literary grasp.

The act of reading is an act of entering another consciousness via language, and perhaps it is the recognition of a voice that brings me back into the dream of reading once again. This tells me that some type of growth is happening inside me, that I'm able to suspend disbelief and escape rather than be bound by my grief-stricken life. There is joy in reading when the reader creates a connection to the writer who somehow has the ability to express something felt or intuitively understood but could never discover the words for oneself. Reading makes a reader feel less alone.

Still, I'm so puzzled to be taken under the spell of *Pioneer Pottery*. I admire so much the efficiency of the prose, but even as he was writing, industry and manufacturing had taken over ceramics. He writes, "There is still something required of a potter if he is to do his work properly—to make useful pots which are at the same time human works of contemporary art." Michael Cardew lived for a time in Africa and opened a pottery there; much of his inspiration for this book came from that experience. He continues, "He must not only trust his own intuitions but he must also have the courage to bring them into the field of conscious thought, and to claim for them the same kind of validity as is enjoyed by the concepts and abstractions used in science. He must live on the frontiers of his art as the scientist lives on the frontiers of his knowledge."

I try to imagine who would read this book, who would be Cardew's intended audience. Or maybe he had no intended audience. Perhaps he simply wrote down everything he knew about opening up a studio and understanding clay. Or is it simply a work of fantasy? I imagine *Pioneer Pottery* as a type of performance art, or a modern novel whose premise is based on the assumption that the reader is looking for a manual to instruct them how to venture into a remote space to build their own pottery from scratch. The concept behind the book, the idea that resonates with me, is that one person is capable of many things, and whether or not you forage into the wild to build your own pottery or to simply build your own life, it's your own obsession that fuels the work. What matters is your own drive, your own power, your own reason to get out of bed each day and lay down your life for what you believe.

Tea

And it is true that even though I am lost and bewildered, the world is still beautiful. The sunrise holds a beautiful light. Thunderous clouds move like silent trains overhead. The birds outside my window fly in circles. In the parking lot of the grocery store, a woman sits alone in her car singing to herself.

Skin

Making a pot is often an exercise in hope and a lesson in failure. And because the process of making a pot goes through several stages, there are many pauses in the making. In these pauses, these breaks in the process, a lot of thinking occurs and hope is employed and failure is feared. It's sort of like planting a garden; you can't help but have hopeful expectations, and yet you can't help having thoughts about how all these little starts could easily perish and die. It's surprising to me to feel hopeful. Right now, I'm thinking about what kind of marks to make on my pots, what the many possibilities entail, and perhaps this is the most exciting part of the process for me so far.

Truthfully though, there's something intimidating that happens when you make a pot and get it ready to do what is known as "decorate." The realm of building with clay disappears, and now there is an emptiness on the surface. The choices feel infinite. What color? What texture? It's sort of like staring at the blank page of a notebook. What to write? What to say? With pots, once you mark the surface of a pot, for example, it's permanent. It's not easy to "erase." My interactions with the clay are recorded, whereas in writing, I can erase everything I write and then write again, and the reader has no idea. The record is harder to trace.

The canvas of the pot feels like the environment where I can be most expressive, less technical. In this arena, I feel the less I know, the better. The pot is a piece of me, and now I have an environment to place my feelings. I can scrawl, I can scratch, I can paint, I can draw, I can glaze, or I can do nothing at all and just leave the clay bare. The goal becomes to not think too hard but to simply feel, to take a risk, to push failure, to make a mark on the pot like a gesture found in nature.

Education

It is the final week of the semester. The final class of the week. Christmas on the horizon. The students have completed most of their work, but the final consists of making a short presentation on something we covered over the course of the fifteen weeks. It's fairly simple and doesn't require much, except that I ask that each student not read from a paper or a screen.

My throat feels sore, my voice scratchy. I'm coming down with the flu once again. I have to say that usually there are good feelings at the end of a class, at least in my experience. But this class is different; all my students look wrecked, zombie-like, in need of a long rest. This is their final class of the final week of school, and most of them haven't prepared very well which is why I give them an easy final.

Each student gives a presentation. We approach the end of the class. The second to last student is a young woman who hasn't attended many classes. There are people in the world who just can't find their way as students, and she is one of them. I've tried to engage her for the entire semester without luck, and now she is here standing before the class and reading from her computer what sounds very obviously like plagiarized writing, but I'm too tired and sick to really object or care. I want this presentation and semester over as much as she does.

Then her phone rings inside her backpack. So all right, I'm used to dealing with devices. We are all used to them interrupting our class, but we march forward and pretend like these events never happened. In this case, the young student walks over to her backpack, finds her phone, and picks it up and answers.

"Hello?" she says. She turns to the class, signaling that she has to excuse herself. She walks out of the classroom and into the hallway to continue her phone conversation. The remaining students turn their heads in my direction. What's going on?

I feel my face flush. I'm angry and tired. I've never witnessed anything like this in a classroom. My fever spikes. I should say something to my students. I should do something right now. A disaster like this can only be salvaged by putting on the breaks, stepping up front and turning this experience into a moment of instruction and learning.

Later, I will recognize the event as more important for my own education, because this is the moment when I realize I can no longer be a teacher in a classroom. Not because of this student, but because I could no longer muster the energy to teach the other students something important about life, about respecting others, about getting along in the world as adults because I am too wrecked, my battery too drained, my interest gone. The time has come for new teachers, new warriors. I understand that my time is done.

Seven

The afternoon before the night my life changed, I am working at home, tucked on my couch, bent over my computer, writing and grading, writing and grading. I alternate between the two worlds. This equation is part of the agreement I have made with myself, part of the bargain of teaching online, a compromise that innocently and stupidly believes that while I am on the computer responding to student questions, I can also be writing a novel.

The skies drizzle at first, and then the rain comes down in sheets. After a spring and summer of drought, the storm carries the first moisture of the season. Earlier in the afternoon, I speak with Julia on the telephone. She is an hour and a half away, working in a cooperative gallery on the coast in the village of Elk. She finishes gallery-sitting in the afternoon. After she closes the gallery, she'll drive home. We talk all the time when we are apart from one another. She describes to me how the ocean looks that afternoon on the Pacific, how theoretically she could see the water from the porch of the gallery. But today the shoreline is covered with fog, so she can't see much except the empty parking lot outside the post office. Seagulls emerge from the mist on the post office roof, then disappear again. There is the sound of the surf, the salty air. She tells me everything is gorgeous and soft.

The gallery, too, is empty; not many people visiting because of the approaching storm, or maybe because there is a television broadcast. A championship game? A playoff? An award show? We don't know. We live separate from the world of mainstream culture. Our friends call us "short-haired hippies" for escaping the city and moving north, but it isn't completely untrue. Julia says she'll close the gallery a little early, get on the road but stop on the way home to pick up ingredients to make a risotto for dinner. I tell her I love her. I return to grading, then fall asleep listening to the rain.

Messengers

When I awake late that afternoon, a blueish light remains in the sky, a mist sprinkling down from a storm that appears to have exhausted itself. Moisture drips from the limbs of pine trees. The space between the studio and cabin reveals puddles of mud. I look through the windows as the last light begins to disappear. My mind cradles a space between dream and wakefulness when I hear something approaching the cabin. Is it a car? Is Julia home early? A momentum draws closer to me, a type of wildness and chaos, but all I can see out my window is gray mist.

Still the sounds grow closer, and they begin to resemble cries. I spot a flurry of dead leaves behind the cabin, and the desperate sounds of panting, heaving, wheezing. What is it? There's something outside my cabin. A mountain lion? A bear? An intense panting circles my cabin, the sound becoming a high-pitched whine.

I am still half asleep; my mind slowed until I see them running up the road through the mist: two dogs headed towards me, chasing each other. Yes, I see these dogs now and this makes sense and comes as a relief, one chasing the other, a black Lab and a yellow Lab, zipping past as I emerge from dream sleep.

Whose dogs are they? I open the door and walk outside onto my deck, looking for signs of the owner, but there is no one but these two Labradors, their coats soaking wet from the rain, frantically running in a loop around Julia's studio and kiln. The atmosphere is charged with frenzy.

They bark, not at me, but at the studio and at each other. They are trying to tell me something else. I feel their distress. Bark. Bark. Bark. They won't stop.

I am awake and watching a movie of myself. I think to give them water. How can I stop these dogs from barking at the studio? Maybe water will help, maybe water will calm them. I put on some shoes and run over to Julia's studio, find two big bowls, and fill them under the tap. Now, I too am breathing hard and feeling panicked. The energy is contagious, like a state of emergency, a shot of electricity. I rest the bowls at the foot of the studio door. When the Labradors circle, they stop this time and look over at me, pink tongues hanging past their chins. Then I understand: these dogs are panicked because they are lost. They don't know where they are.

The Labs hover near me, then bend to drink the water from the bowls, lapping up the sides with gusto. I see tags on their collars. On one tag is a phone number. The black Lab is called "Speed," and the yellow one "Lightning." I bring the water inside Julia's studio, and the dogs follow me. As soon as they're inside, I close the door.

Being inside the studio seems to create a state of calm. The dogs sniff around the room, taking a temperature of the place.

It's like they're just beginning to focus after running around in circles where everything around them was spinning. The black Lab allows me to pet him. He sinks to the floor at my feet, followed shortly by the other.

I read the number on the collar and go to retrieve my phone back in the cabin. I feel almost excited, my adrenaline flowing from their whirlwind arrival. The skies have turned completely dark.

I glance at the clock and estimate that Julia is driving on her way home from the gallery. I can't wait to call her, but her phone won't be in range. I want to tell her about these dogs, to describe to her what is happening. What time is it now? I have schoolwork to complete before the end of the day, before Julia gets home. It is getting dark, and more rain moves overhead. When is Julia coming home?

Parallax View

I live side by side with roughly eight hundred pieces of pottery. Not all of them are in my cabin; most reside outside in the woods. Others are down by the fence that leads to the creek. Many are stacked in the studio, shelved on ware carts or tucked away in boxes. Some glisten like jewels; others survive as mistakes with broken handles or wounded lids littered on the outskirts of my garden. In the beginning of my grief, I clung to every shard while simultaneously sensing the overwhelming weight of my collection of pots.

When I met Julia, the world changed in proportion because of the way we moved together as a couple. Love is a potent hallucinogenic; you see and hear things when you're in love that you can't experience alone. Throwing pots on the wheel gradually brought me to a new understanding with my eight hundred pots. The experience was an emotional parallax, sensing my collection from two perspectives. The pots didn't change positions; it was me, moving through my own life while working with clay on the wheel. Now, when I approach a shelf to choose a bowl to use, I see the pot as a reminder of what has been lost, but I also view the bowl as my teacher, my confidant, my reservoir of love.

Production

I have been told to throw six versions of one form. For example, throw six pitchers, then six bowls. It's a type of discipline to train your hands to work with clay, but also as a discipline for your eyes to look closely at form.

I am making a lot of work. The more experience I get on the wheel, the more confident I am guiding the clay where I want. Often the pots are too heavy, or sometimes a little tipsy, but I keep pushing forward. I learn to trash work that isn't any good, re-wedge the clay, and try again. That's all I do. I keep trying. There's a fearlessness I have at the moment, and I recognize what freedom it gives me when working in clay. Something about the material gives me confidence. I feel like I can make anything, and it doesn't matter. It is a feeling I have never felt as a writer.

Maybe it's because I don't think with my hands in clay. I don't judge, I don't edit, I don't sit back and see what's wrong unless it's obvious. I don't have time; the clay needs attention. I just work.

Unbearable

You might think grief is a type of depression. The mood arrives and hovers like an overcast sky. Indeed, there's an aspect to grief that is fog-soaked and gloomy, the perfect climate for crawling into bed and waiting for darkness to pass. But grief shows up on luminous days, when creeks run fast, when skies radiate blue. Grief happens inside the back seat of cars speeding through intersections. Grief blooms on those days when you lose track of yourself, when you forget the pain enough to relax and have a good time. In the end, grief never leaves. It never goes away. So how to bear the unbearable that never leaves? The mystery of any pot lies within the durability of clay, the regenerative qualities of the earth.

Building

A teapot is one of the most challenging objects to create in clay because it combines many different skills that need to come together in just the right proportion to make a teapot that is any good. I make a lot of teapots, but they never work right, or they look awkward and unsteady. This is a story about failure, about putting pieces together and forming them into a whole that is both functional and expressive.

Step One: Form the Body

There is beauty in my grief-stricken world that doesn't include me. And while I grieve, part of me stands outside the rest of the world, separate from all that previous joy. This morning the sun rises just over the Mayacamas to the east. For no particular reason, the atmosphere hangs over me with regret, but the air is electrified and filled with love. I can't see it, but I know it's there.

I feel safe inside the clay studio. It's just clay, after all. And I have this incredible feeling of freedom when I work with clay in the studio because I'm trying to make a map of this new world and I'm looking and searching for the parameters of clay. What can I do with a mound of dirt? How far can I go? What can't I do? What are the limits? My job is simply to learn, to be open, to find the parameters of the clay and my own desires. That's all.

Step Two: Form the Spout

There are days when I don't recognize myself, when I'm grinding down pots after a firing and I'll think for a moment about what I'm doing. At a certain point in my life, I thought my identity was pretty solid: I was a teacher and a writer. I read a lot of books. I used to do a lot of swimming. I used to spend time in restaurants. I used to do things like go on vacation. I used to never be alone. I was a husband. A lover. What I never understood is that identity is fluid in so many ways, and what we see of ourselves and how others observe us quickly changes and transforms over time. And yet, we insist we are always the same, no matter what. We insist on something that is not possible. I can no longer insist that I stay the same or that others stay the same because I know the truth to be otherwise. If we're alive, we're moving and changing.

Step Three: Form the Lid

Forgetting doesn't mean memories disappear; the memories move out of sight, they become more well-hidden. Memories are the surviving pieces that remain, and yet I can't hold on to all of these pieces. There isn't enough room inside me to carry all these memories and try to function day-to-day. So I begin to forget, I begin to shed memories in little chunks, struggling to recall names, piecing together chronologies, the shape of her face, the place where our van broke down. Forgetting comes with residual guilt. What can I do? I rent out a storage space in town. I put clothes and pots and journals and photo albums inside a metallic shed that is nestled inside a row of similar container spaces, an exiled world outside my own exile. For eighty dollars a month I pay rent so I won't have to view the contents of my own memories. I feel as if this is a really good deal and frees up room in the clay studio.

Step Four: Form the Handle

Love can be a type of fuel in the world, propelling us forward, and so when there is a lack of love, there is a slowing down of the world, a halting of the momentum of life. I'm afraid of falling in love again, afraid of becoming that vulnerable to the world. I understand love can heal. There are many different types of love in the world, and I feel as if art has taken over that part of me. My passion for art has become my way to connect, my way to relate to the world, my way to give and receive love.

Final Step: Putting It All Together

How well the individual pieces are constructed doesn't matter. What matters most is how they join, how they connect and what they express as a whole. There will never be a smoothness to my life, a veneer that is polished and vibrant. My life is full of holes, pieces strung and attached with epoxy and glue, moments of change balancing precariously from day to day.

Sprint

I have made enough pots of my own to fire the kiln. This is the first time I've fired it all by myself. I hope nothing goes wrong, but I brace myself for disaster. My making of pots has graduated into the arena of obsession, craziness, and compulsion. I focus on making as many pots as I can so I can fill the kiln. I can't work fast enough. It's almost as if I want to make these pots to get these pots out of the way, to produce them as a way of expelling them in order to make room for the pots I really want to make.

My dream is that one of the pots that emerges from this kiln will be a beautiful pot, even though I understand art is slow and patient, and I can't force the kiln to produce beautiful pots. Nevertheless, I can't stop myself from hoping.

I am operating a propane-fueled kiln with eight burners beneath it, flames coming up through ports in the base and rising from the chimney. The kiln sometimes sounds like it's muffling other sounds, voices or songs, a combination of a crowded beach against a faraway surf. The heat builds all day long until it is too hot to stand within close proximity. I am reading the temperature on the pyrometer, tracking the heat as it marches upwards until I finally meet temperature and shut the kiln down.

I am in a state of disbelief that I somehow lit and fired a sixteen cubic foot kiln to twenty-three hundred degrees over a twelve-hour period. All I had to do was follow Julia's notes and turn up the gas at different intervals. It sounds easy, but it's different working a tool like heat and not really understanding the properties of heat or how heat works. I still don't know how the kiln works without collapsing or exploding. After it cools, I open the door, feeling a wave of heat over my face. I scour the shelves to see what pots survived, to see the results of having thrown these pots on the wheel and made glazes for their surfaces. But when I lift my first pots out of the kiln, I am taken back. I don't recognize these pots at all.

What happened? Who made these bowls?

In my mind, I etched an image of what these pots would look like when they emerged, but in real life they are far different. They are mostly brown. They look burnt. A few of them look stuck to the shelf. But there's also a glimmer, something inside the kiln that reflects light. The pots feel miraculous because now they are solid. And now that they are out of the kiln, the pots belong to themselves. The pots begin their own journey.

"Weird," a friend says to me later. "Your pots look exactly like Julia's pots." Another friend makes the same comment. I am showing my pots to everyone. I'm eager to learn, excited to share what feels insurmountable. The similarities make most of my friends uncomfortable. But I know it isn't Julia making those pots "through me." Rather, these pots show the influence of half a lifetime with a potter and watching her work. Julia,

I realize, is my first pottery teacher. The relationship keeps changing.

My friend tells me I need to relax. There's no reason to want so much so fast. Life is a marathon, my friend says. Ceramics takes time. You still have a long way to go.

I know my friend is right, his advice sound. But I feel the opposite. I feel there is a very short way to go, and if there is any time to sprint, the time is now.

THE SOLID STATE

Definition: The Solid State

The clay has been transformed through heat, a synthesis of science and art, a snapshot of consciousness caught and captured in the midst of a swirling universe.

But, like all states, the solid state is temporary. Pots fall down and break. Pots get lost in the world. Eventually, all pots move beyond the solid state and enter an invisible form.

Vases

INTERIOR: STUDIO

Time-lapse begins with the sun streaming from the east.

In an empty ceramic studio, seven vases sit on a table in a horizontal line from left to right.

The soundtrack begins with silence, but gradually we hear voices talking, maybe voices that belong to people who live next door, upstairs, in the basement. The light moves slowly across the studio and over the rims of the vases. We hear sirens racing past. The sound of pipes, footsteps on stairs. Voices seem to inhabit the vases. The words and meaning are remote, mechanical, declarative, lacking emotion.

The camera pans across the vases, mimicking the passing of the sun: early morning, noon, late afternoon, dusk, darkness.

Replenishment

I have never eaten liver, but at a certain point, I crave it. I am not in my body; I am floating in the air above myself, inside my head, neglecting my body. The vehicle is breaking down, but this body of mine fights back, wrestling control of my health and not bothering to explain. It wants liver.

It's a cold summer day in Daly City; the fog whips over the parking lot at Westlake Joe's, not far from Lake Merced. I am sitting at the counter eating liver and ravioli, observing the cooks behind the counter as they work in rapid-fire to fill orders. The people at the counter are all smiles because the food is good, priced reasonably, and the atmosphere is like watching a play from the wings of the stage. Waiters, busboys in white shirts and black ties, an expediter calling out orders, heat lamps, char-broiler, the slate of onions caramelizing in front of me. It feels like cheating being here without Julia, but I tell myself not to feel guilty, to understand she would probably want me to eat well, to take better care of myself.

However, the fact that I am eating out, ordering drinks and eating liver when I have no job and no plan as to how I'm going to survive because I can't see myself going back to teach again is proof that I'm still in the land of bewilderment, still impervious to normal concerns.

A man next to me at the counter starts narrating how he comes here every Thursday. I don't know why this older man believes he can just start talking to me, but I notice people seem to open up, strangers and circumstances flowing through me like a window flung open. Maybe people sense the opening in me, the missing part. Or maybe it's because I'm single, alone, no longer part of a couple, no longer hermetically sealed with a lover, but now open to the world in a different way.

My neighbor orders the Steak a la Bruno and an extra side of steamed veggies.

"The best steak," he says. He's in his seventies, bald, retired. He's wearing a windbreaker with an insignia of the 49ers covering a collared shirt. It's four-thirty in the afternoon, just before the dinner time rush. Being around people having a good time boosts my spirits as long as I don't have to join in. I feel the heat from the ovens, the grill. My neighbor tells me that he comes here every week because he doesn't know how to cook.

"Me neither," I say.

Once a week he comes to Joe's for a decent meal. Takes the rest home for leftovers. He points to two gentlemen sitting next to him. They are older like him, one eating chicken piccata, the other the pork chop. They nod at me, but I don't think they can hear very well. The three of them meet here every week to check in on each other.

"We're widowers," he says. "And terrible cooks."

The counter erupts in laughter; he's told this joke before. I look down at my plate. The liver is broiled and comes with bacon, so if you cut the pieces up and lather them up with meat sauce, you don't have to experience that strange metallic aftertaste that comes with eating liver. I've never experienced the feeling of craving a food whose taste I disliked, but there are a lot of things about myself I don't recognize, places I find myself where I don't know how I arrived. But I'm here, and I'm hungry.

Haywire

Pots tell stories, some of them literal and some of them more abstract. They tell stories in a way language can't outwit. The pot contains an interior life as well as an exterior existence. Exactly where edges begin and end is not so clear. There's nothing sequential about the story of a pot. It's happening in the past, present, future, all at once, simultaneously.

On one channel, a pot tells the story of its maker. On another channel, the pot tells the story of the earth. On another channel, when I examine a pot, I'm looking for signs of a story I didn't witness but can only imagine. I see the results of a performance I didn't observe, notes from a moment of awakening. The serving bowl is a document of the maker's energy, a mirror to a performance of art.

The beauty is that a pot is open-ended. A new person engages with a pot when they encounter it on a kitchen table or fireplace mantel. Even when a pot falls and breaks, those shards of clay continue the narration, albeit in broken, fragmented form. Many times, when we look at pots, we stand apart from them in order to judge. I think the better approach is to step closer to them and absorb the many stories these pots have to tell.

Grief is a type of estrangement from the normal narrative. Cause and effect appear random and not causative at all. The storyline has gone haywire. And you realize that the narrative trajectory of your own life is false; you've misled yourself through your own dreams and ambitions, becoming blind to your own self-stories. The floor has become the ceiling; the valley has become the mountain; the edges blur. But more importantly, this haywire narrative is only one story, your own story that no one can enter except you. Grief brings out the gray areas between the interior and the exterior, so beginnings and endings blur with a new intensity. In that way, I'm more like a pot, someone made of many stories all happening simultaneously, occurring right now, all at once.

Swimming

When I first learn to throw pots, I experience clay as if I am swimming in a lake surrounded by mountains, in depths warmed by the sun, water so clear I can see rocks on the bottom. I keep swimming and swimming, getting myself used to the lakewater, learning what I can do, how far I can swim. So much of swimming in lakes has to do with psychology and always wondering how far I am from shore. I become a stronger swimmer and more confident to swim further in the lake. My swimming becomes another obsession, a way to ward off grief by tiring myself out. One day, in the middle of the lake, I decide to think about where I am swimming. I consider where I want to go as if I were traveling on a journey. Now everything changes. Swimming isn't just swimming; swimming isn't exercise; it's a vehicle for direction. I have the ability to choose where I want to swim.

That's the moment when I begin to think of myself as a maker of objects and not just a thrower of pots.

Reclaim

Clay reinvents itself at every stage, the material used and reused over and over again. All the mistakes on the wheel are tossed into a bucket of scraps. The trimmings and carvings of the pots are scooped and deposited inside the bucket to be reused. Plates that develop cracks are dismissed into the reclaim bucket, including the slop at the bottom of the splash pan, the clay gathered on my fingers and arms, the dried clay caked to my tools. All of it is recycled and used again. When the bucket fills, I add water and let it slake down into a muddy slip. Once I get the slip to be the texture of thick yogurt, I pour the bucket onto a plaster slab to dry the contents, eventually wedging the clay into balls of material I can once again use on the wheel.

And so on and so on.

I recognize this reclaim clay when I'm using it once again to form a bowl or throw a pot. I imagine the person who I was just months ago touching this same dirt. Something is different. It's like looking at snapshots caught in the midst of making, and I'm realizing that the pull of clay has deepened within me. I get lost in clay and don't worry about where I'm going or how I will get wherever I'm supposed to go. I still think of clay as Julia's domain, her place for art, but clay has made its way into my life as well. What's the point of telling myself that clay is just a hobby when the attraction to the material tells me clay is more than just a balm to my life? Why should I pretend it's not there?

It's liberating to think I can recycle my mistakes, that I can absorb all those failures and doubts, that by adding water, breaking them down, wedging and forming them into something else, I can transform my mistakes into an object on a kitchen table or a vase sitting on a mantle. I question my own sanity, knowing that making pots is not a way to make a living, that the work is physical and back-breaking at times. Despite those concerns, it just makes more sense to listen to the clay and how it speaks to me, to let the clay shape my life and let go of any expectations or worries about my future.

Farmer's Market

On Saturday mornings, I rise before the sun, pack my car with pots, folding tables, and a red market umbrella. The sky lightens from charcoal gray to powder. Setting up a booth to sell creates a quiet storm of panic inside me. The temperature already tips upward to seventy-five degrees as the sun rises. As I load my car, a single rivulet of sweat runs down the center of my back. I remind myself what I will need for the day: my receipt book, freshly cut flowers for the vases, a bottle of water, a hat to shield me from the sun, a bottle of aspirin, a pen to write. I remember to pack signs, a white covering for my table, my clipboard email list, some fresh fruit to eat between moments with customers.

When the car has been packed, I drive down-valley toward the local farmer's market to set up my ceramic wares on folding tables and boxes. I tell myself over and over how much I enjoy selling at the farmer's market because believing that theory makes selling easier. I've taken these pots from a lump of clay, formed them with my hands, fired them in a kiln, sanded them, packed them, and now escort them the final distance towards their original purpose: to venture out into the world and to be of use in someone else's life. Each week I summon the energy to convince random human beings to buy pots and make them part of their own worlds, to look at handmade plates and bowls as something just as nourishing on their kitchen tables as fresh market vegetables or just-baked sourdough bread. This is my purpose now; this is why I find myself getting up at the crack of dawn.

I will admit that taking my pots to market this morning makes me feel something that leans in the direction of joy. Never in my writing life have I presented my work in public, stood next to it, and listened to strangers make comments ("It's awfully heavy" or "Can you make this mug in red?"), yet I feel immune and free. There's no hiding from yourself when you put all of your artwork on a table and have it priced to sell; the market booth is a place of truth and vulnerability. I never know what's going to happen, who will approach my booth, or how they will react.

I now think of selling pots as a type of performance art. There are stretches of time while standing in my booth looking out at all of my colleagues selling bottles of olive oil, fresh cheese, tomato-starts, and bouquets of flowers when I feel like a player on a stage or an "extra" on a movie set. I see myself within the larger landscape, inside the aisles of the farmer's market where people walk around simply looking, enjoying the day, stepping out of their lives and poking around.

A customer approaches my table and looks down at my table of mugs. She's looking for a cup with a handle that will work for her arthritic hands. We have a discussion about the subtleties of a handle or whether to grab the cup with one hand or two. I'm learning how to sell to a customer, how to build a relationship with them with my pots. We pick up every mug, and she tries them all; she needs a handle that can fit her whole hand, but the mug can't be too heavy. We discover a mug that is suitable, but then she says to me, "I can't buy anything today. I have too much stuff already." I agree with her that she has too much stuff already, and the moment is over. I've failed at the crucial time to finish the sale, but I'm torn about pushing too hard with my work. It's a delicate balance.

I like to tell myself that I'm no longer a teacher, but in order to sell a pot I have to bring some education to people who want to use handmade pots. The real education, however, is mine standing in a parking lot every Saturday morning presenting my work to the world. When I go back to the studio, I come with new information, new feedback. People seem to like my pots, but there are some aspects they don't like. Strangers tell me stories about their favorite bowl or the time they took a class on ceramics in high school. The writer in me loves hearing these stories, listening to the way people speak and the feelings they have for handmade objects.

All morning I have not made one sale. Then suddenly, in the last half hour of the market, a flurry of customers. There's an element of shock when a customer decides to buy pieces of my pottery. I wrap them in newspaper and put these pots in a paper bag. I watch my former clay pots leave the parking lot and disappear into the world, and I am moved and surprised at the feeling inside me.

I am becoming a potter because I want to bring pots to people, to connect with my community with handmade objects. My own will becomes manifest because I have found an outlet to bring my pots into the world, in a setting that is outdoors under natural light, free for anyone to come and visit, and a chance for me to talk about what is important in my life.

Minimalism

Composing a sentence requires many passes set at oddly paced intervals, reading the sentence back to myself to arrange the words in the right order, combining ideas to make the ideas flow together, and absorbing how the sentences "read" together inside the arena of a paragraph. I'm fascinated by how we read. Sometimes we read to get to the end, to finish the thought, the paragraph, the story, the novel, as if the sentence becomes a method of transport delivering us to a new geography of the mind. Sometimes, however, the journey fascinates me more. I love to linger in a beautifully written sentence, to let go of my own expectations of clarity and reward and simply bask in the courage of language.

I live with handmade pots, and using them is like reading. These pots become part of my knowledge base for making my own work. I am learning the perfect weight of a cup in my hand or the small detail hidden at the foot of a bowl. It's not necessarily that the pot is beautiful to me, or that the pot works so well and fits my hand so perfectly; often I get lost thinking about the person who made the pot or puzzle about how the pot was made.

Parking Lot

It is lunchtime. We meet at the gray beach where we sit inside K's car and eat from brown paper bags balanced precariously on our laps. Thursdays come too infrequently. There is nothing we can do with our guilt except to indulge it. The parking lot sits mostly empty while waves curl against the horizon, wind lifting the wings of seagulls and swirling awkward gusts of fog. We sit like tourists lost in love-transit, eating crackers and cream cheese, sipping beer and biting on the corners of tuna-fish sandwiches. Is this love? I wonder, and maybe K is too. Hoping doesn't make it so.

We bond through grief, at counseling sessions where we met six months ago. Now we have created our own support group that feels more like dating. K's husband died from bladder cancer. I lost my wife two years ago. K is my age. She is the first person who understands me and the grief that won't leave me. She is brave and courageous. She knows how precious this life is. I didn't know I could feel this way again.

We squint through the drizzled windshield while making up stories about people wrapped in coats and scarves, cleaning up after their incontinent dogs. We decipher the dreary graffiti sprayed on the cement barriers, the man with the headphones and the blankets he uses to protect his cats from the cold wet. The banter between us comes so easily. We both wonder why we find satisfaction eating potato chips and drinking beers while staring into the frothy ocean surf, but we do. We can't deny it.

Is this love? Doesn't it happen just like this? I don't feel qualified to answer. Grief can make the most impossible thing feel possible.

Later, I walk back to my car, turn the ignition, and drive back to the studio. I wanted to kiss her, but I worried about the sweat and the smell of my body, my clothes full of clay dust. Grief is an aphrodisiac, but there's a part of me that's awkward and unsure of myself. I warned K how dangerous it might be to be around someone who doesn't understand his own capabilities.

On the other side of town, the fog dissipates, the skies open, the painted yellow lines pop in contrast to the black pavement. I meet friends at a restaurant. I'm focusing on the bowls on the table, how they were made, determining if they were mass-produced or individually thrown. Outside, the streets appear so straight and clear in the tangerine light of late afternoon.

In-Between

I keep moving, never keeping still. I relocate back to the city temporarily. I stay with friends, couch surf, camp in the woods, sleep in my car. I am starting to write again in my journal by sitting at picnic tables in campgrounds or public parks. I am surprised by how much space my friends give me, how generous they are to me. Grieving has given me permission to do whatever I please. I have become more connected to my friends in a more intimate way; their confessions to me, sharing details of their relationships, shedding the pretense that everything is always "fine." On a certain level, I am in awe of how grief sharpens the dullness that blurs the pretense of our lives.

I accept the fact that the world comes to me now in the shape of pots. I tell my friends that sometimes I feel like a bowl. We laugh because my obsession with pots is out of control. Just because I feel crazy doesn't mean I don't see the humor. But the truth is friends and total strangers confess their deepest fears to me, share their own stories of grief. I don't know if this is normal, if it's something about me, about my hunger to understand what happened, but I feel defenseless against this outpouring. Instead of trying to resist, I give in. I say yes to everything and everyone. I hurl myself from one place to another.

To be alone, I get in my car and drive north. I love the feeling of beginnings, the start of a road trip, the feeling of shedding the world with each distant mile. I find myself in a private campground just north of Eureka. I am there to walk in the Redwoods and hike to the ocean. It's gray and late in the afternoon. Private campgrounds are different from state parks. This campground is more like a parking lot with a lot of trees and a "fun" room for kids. I have no choice; there are no other places to camp this evening, so I enter the camp headquarters and pay for a space to park my Toyota. I fill out a postcard with my name, address, and license plate. The final question asks me for my occupation. I write: Potter.

I find a spot and back my Toyota into my space. I do not have a tent; I usually sleep in the back of my Toyota with the seats down and a foam pad. This is my floating apartment. The campsite is off to the side and shielded by a giant Redwood tree. I know that I have to wake up the following day under this Redwood, so I decide to sleep under the stars. Already I have fallen under the spell of this tree, so I spread a tarp and lay out on my sleeping bag. I eat a sandwich, drink a beer, and fall asleep. It is dark underneath the Redwoods, the canopy of leaves blocking the moon and the stars.

Trimming

If a pot is too heavy, you can lighten it by trimming away some of the extra clay. It's important to remember that when I make a pot it's in a continuous state of change. It feels like my pots need my attention constantly because they transform so quickly. There's always something going on with a pot, even when I'm not there to see it.

Think of trimming pots like the peeling of a potato, but going deeper toward the core. If I think of myself as a pot revolving on a wheel, and life as the knife that cuts the fat, I can understand that grief is the implement of the moment and that the pain is part of the experience of change, the sculpting away of all that is extra. And when I think of trimming a pot, I'm not just thinking of making the pot lighter; I'm thinking about the new shape revealed, the hidden form come to life.

Whales

I have been an English major for most of my life, but I have somehow avoided Hawthorne and Melville. I have taken classes in literature that covered *The Scarlet Letter* or *Billy Budd*, but I never read them because I was the type of English major who didn't do all the reading. I have always been more interested in European novelists, South American novelists, and modern novelists, but not many American novelists from the traditional canon.

One morning I wake up at four o'clock, remember that Julia is gone, and then go back to bed. In my dreams, I'm walking along the shore, on a hilltop overlooking the sea. The air is cold, and I see something outside, to the west of me, swimming along the shore. It's a whale. And then I wake up. I am in my bed, alone, nowhere near the ocean.

That afternoon, I find a copy of *Moby Dick* by Herman Melville on my bookshelf. I read the first two hundred pages and then set the book down. This is the first book of fiction I have read in over two years. I didn't think I would be able to concentrate, but something happens to me inside the pages of *Moby Dick*. I can't describe it in words, but one thing is for sure: I don't want to read this book too fast. I want to enjoy it, savor it, spread it out over weeks, months, years. Afterwards, I walk into the clay studio, make some space on the work table, and begin to sculpt a whale.

I have never sculpted, never wanted to make something so specific as a whale, but I begin coiling and pinching, shaping and coaxing the clay into the shape of a whale. After two weeks, my first whale arrives in my studio, and I am startled that something so strange would come out of me and be manifest in sculpture. I sense a gear inside me click, shift, move.

I quickly begin to make another whale.

And then another whale.

And another.

For the next few years, I make whales while I make pots. I don't know where exactly these whales originate, if they come from the pages of *Moby Dick* or from my own dreams. I don't know if these whales are beautiful or ugly, whether they are art or non-art, but it doesn't matter. I have no judgment of these whales, and I accept them into my life without understanding why. It occurs to me that one of the biggest challenges of writing for me was judging my own writing, critiquing my words before they were even written. With clay, I have a freedom I lacked as a writer, an openness and a willingness to take risks and to follow my own instincts. And I think to myself: if there ever comes a day when I return to writing, I want to have this feeling; I want to write with the same curiosity and belief that I have when I'm sculpting whales.

One day, a visitor to the studio asks me about the origination of the whales in my practice, and I mention *Moby Dick*. I tell him that I have stopped asking why I'm making whales and just accept the gifts of their presence when I receive them.

I see the whales through the visitor's eyes, and it's clear to me that my visitor sees all art as autobiographical, something self-revealing. I've never seen art as strictly autobiographical, but if you had the kind of perspective my visitor had, I could understand how the whales might appear to be self-portraits, snapshots of me, migrating through waters of grief.

Hope

I think good teachers take their own advice, but probably many teachers say one thing and do something else entirely. I'm speaking for myself, but one of the things I told my writing students was that I was not an expert, not a pro. My writing life felt like walking inside a blizzard of words, unformed ideas attempting to make their way forward. I didn't say this explicitly (maybe I should have), but I really have no idea what I am doing when writing. I know a few things, but most of it I am learning on the fly.

However, deep inside I expect myself to have control and mastery, to write beautiful prose effortlessly. Even though I told my students to be kind to their first drafts, I wasn't. I was harsh because I felt frustrated. I enter the page expecting all the elements to come together quickly as I type and then discover how awkward and cumbersome it is to work with language.

But the thing is that even though I know it's hard work and mostly failure, when I first start to write I have that same optimism, that same belief that the words will flow. And I'm thinking to myself that perhaps being a writer teaches you so much, but especially about failure. Writing gives one experience with disaster; it's how you handle the tragedies inside your sentence that describes what kind of writer you are. At the same time, you have to be slightly cracked to sit down to write. A person like this possesses a naive optimism each time he or she approaches a sentence, fails at the endeavor, and then returns the next moment, the next hour, the next day for more of the same.

Quartz Inversion

In French cooking, there is the cassoulet, a stew of meats and vegetables cooked over a long period of time, sometimes years. You can't measure the experience of eating a bowl of cassoulet. Same with firing a pot in a kiln. A kiln is not just an "oven." Kilns are built to be fired to a high temperature over a period of time. The way to measure heat in a kiln is to look at temperature and time.

And the same goes with marriage. It's hard to explain how a marriage works, how a relationship can endure and not suddenly explode and dismantle itself. Love is never static or remaining still. What sparks at the beginning is only a hint of what will be built over time.

In that sense, love is the heat inside the kiln. Over time the heat increases, until it doesn't. I understand that my relationship with Julia is changing: our marriage is over. There's a part of me that has to divorce myself from the marriage, a difficult thing to do by oneself, but I know there's nothing I can do to stop the flame from extinguishing.

When one half dies, the kiln can't continue to fire, the source of the heat is no longer, and slowly, over time, the temperature falls until the kiln reaches room temperature. At that point, the door to the kiln can be opened (brick by brick), and even then you'll feel some residual heat, but the pots should be cool enough to touch.

Satellite

A contractor arrives to fix the satellite dish. Living in a remote area, I need a good internet connection. I am working quietly by myself in the studio when a van drives up the road. I haven't seen a human being in days. Roberto introduces himself, and I show him the satellite dish. He inches back from my cabin and turns his head to the skies. He paces on my deck, stopping and looking up. He tells me he used to work in the cable industry.

Roberto says it is hard to find clear air space, not only because of the trees around my cabin but also because of the shadow of the trees. I haven't counted on the shadows of the trees being a factor, but I know what he is saying. From his pocket he pulls a receiver that shoots a beam of light into the sky, searching for an uninterrupted line to the satellite floating over us.

"How far up is it?" I ask. He says satellites fly at 20,000 miles above the earth.

I stay quiet while he recalibrates my satellite dish. So much depends on the coordinates. For a moment, Roberto reminds me that I inhabit a planet revolving around a sun. Everything around us and above us vibrates in constant motion. Sometimes

I get so lost in my head making pots I forget I am breathing air and resisting the pull of gravity. I need to be like that instrument; a receiver pointed up at the sky. And it isn't just the trees blocking, but their shadows hovering over me.

Strength

You don't necessarily need to be strong to throw pots. Working with clay will make your hands and wrists naturally stronger, but I think it's a myth that muscle strength is a necessity.

What is necessary is a type of inner fortitude, a resiliency to remain quiet and still during the ebbs and tides of storms. I think of my hands as creating an outside wall, and that nothing will move those hands no matter how bumpy the ride gets. Strength requires a type of resoluteness to remain faithful to yourself no matter what ensues.

Another way to look at it is to reconsider the idea that throwing pots requires muscle and consider instead the notion that throwing pots requires leadership. The clay is lost on the wheel, searching for a place to land, a form to inhabit. The torque of the wheel flings the clay outwards, but the clay doesn't necessarily want to go there. That's where you come in; that's where your hands provide the leadership to guide the clay firmly up into the air.

The way I show my strength is to build an invisible wall with my hands. Nothing can permeate this wall, not even the clay. This is what I intend, but it turns out that if I am honest and truthful, I find growth through all my inconsistencies, all my weaknesses. And through invention and creativity, make these faults into art.

Loneliness

Growing up, I developed the ability to be alone with others. All four of us children were raised as independent units, sibling-nonsiblings, subletters in an Irish-Catholic household in the California suburbs, where all the anger and resentment was mute until it exploded, until one of the lodgers got caught sneaking out of the house, stealing, lying, or doing drugs.

The atmosphere was quiet for a house full of kids, in large part because we were fearful of making our mother sick with a headache. Of course, our mother was a loner. A question that was never answered was why our parents decided to have four children. She suffered from migraines, kept the living room drapes drawn and the house dark. Bright lights and loud voices could trigger one of her week-long clusters. There was no screaming in our house, no yelling, no running around. She felt outnumbered when we gathered together, so she played each sibling against the other. When she got one of her migraines, she made sure to blame one of us in particular. The guilt would pierce me in half. On one of our walls hung a picture of John F. Kennedy, and in the pantry, a version of St Francis's Prayer painted on a varnished wooden slab. There were no pictures of us.

What does it mean to be a loner? It's a type of contentment in the world not dependent on others. Loners believe in self-reliance. Our mother would say: Go to your room and be quiet. Her strategy worked in the short-term, but then came the fights, the inevitable showdowns, the rebellions. The headaches and clashes became worse when we reached high school.

At eighteen I left home for good, relieved of the burden of family, all that quiet, all that silence. The idea of living in a dorm seemed surreal. I lived with roommates through college and tried to live as a non-loner in a non-loner world. I worked as a waiter and forced myself to have fun around other people, but I didn't have the energy for it. My first studio apartment was in the basement of a brownstone on Beacon Street in Boston. The windows looked into an alley, and I slept on a mattress on the floor. Despite how far I had run from home, I was still that same lodger who required time alone. Each evening I sat down at my desk and wrote.

There is a difference between being alone and being truly alone. There are days that I never leave my house, yet I've talked on the phone, corresponded in a way that makes my day seem lively, as if I've been far away. There are days when I never leave the house and I turn off my phone. There are days when I never leave the house and I forget I have a phone—and on those days, when I'm truly alone and not feeling pulled by any outside source—I feel truly blessed and fortunate.

But there are days when being alone feels unbearable. I find myself running into walls. I keep expecting something to appear, but nothing does. The solitude becomes oppressive. Solitude leaves no screen between you and the rest of the world. There's nothing around to distract, and sometimes the self-focus can feel strangling. It's important to be active if you live your life alone, to be physical in some way every day, because if you end up living most of the time in your head, it's going to get weird.

How do you become a writer? You begin by retreating inward. Writing as an action, as a pure exertion, is a thing of prolonged interior concentration. Books and poems are the result of an intense use of the brain to create and communicate ideas from one consciousness to another. You have to get your brain into good shape in order to make something big, like a novel or a poem. That kind of precise and penetrating concentration takes years to build. But the initial impulse, to search within, is the first step in writing.

To concentrate, to practice concentrating for something like being a writer, you need a space and time to practice. How hard is it to retreat from our daily dissonant lives and into the quiet world of imagination and composition? Try sitting with yourself for an hour with no distractions. Just you and your thoughts. See what that's like.

What's difficult is thinking of yourself in terms of a couple and then thinking of yourself in terms of just you. The world of couples and families belongs to couples and families. I remember a friend telling her teenage daughter: you can't have two best friends. They'll end up hating each other. Just pick one and the other one can hate you. But don't involve an innocent.

My friend speaks to her teenager like this, and it makes sense to me. Single people throw the balance off. Why are you alone? Don't you need somebody with you? How are you going to get home? Do you have a ride?

I don't think it's a good idea to avoid loneliness. I might meet loneliness in a crowd of family or in the middle of a medical waiting room. Sometimes I feel lonely navigating touch tone menus (Press zero to speak to an operator). It's painful to feel the truth, to stare at it and find a way to get more at ease with it. It's not being alone that's so hard; it's being afraid of being alone.

Hands

My hands need the practice mostly. I'm not used to this kind of heavy work, but touching clay brings me to an intuitive place beyond my rational brain. The clay opens up a vein that seems to be more natural to me than I expected. Even right now, I would prefer to have my hands shaping clay rather than poised over a keyboard.

The brain and the hands work together to become more agile and responsive. Time creates the deepest bonds. Now, when I touch clay, I'm much more gentle. I'm not so bullish—knocking things down or breaking things off. Somewhere in the process of holding on and letting go, I've conjured a softness in my hands.

In a way, my story is the story of my hands, how at one point they were empty and awkward, but now they have transformed my life and introduced me to clay, the touch of dirt and watery slip. I feel late to this understanding of myself, and I desire to make up for lost time, trying to make up for all those years I was ignorant of clay. It's as if I have very little time left for myself, and I know I have to use this remaining life as intelligently as possible. The more I work, the more responsive my own hands become to clay. But not just clay—to everything else around me. Using my hands gives me a certain confidence.

It's personal and private to talk about my hands because hands are capable of so many things that a person may be ignorant of, perhaps due to a lack of experience or an absence of courage. Sometimes my hands go where they want to go without letting me know. They move about the clay sometimes out of boredom, sometimes hoping to find a new solution before I can even imagine what the obstacle or problem might be.

Beauty

In order to throw beautiful pots, I search for the place between holding on and letting go. Holding on means controlling the clay, throwing it where I want to throw it, manipulating the edges of the clay to points directed by me and expressed with my hands. Holding on enforces my will on the clay to the best of my abilities.

At a certain point, I let go of the clay. I take it off the wheel. I leave it to dry. The next day I trim it. Then, I bisque fire to make it hard enough so I can decorate it. Then I fire the clay again to vitrify the surface and body. Then, hopefully, I take it to market where a customer takes a liking to the pot and decides to buy it. At that point, I wrap the pot in newspaper and write up a receipt. It is at that point when I finally let go.

But not really.

Pots have a way of coming back into my life. I can't control or predict the journey of a pot once it leaves my hands. There's always an element of letting go through the entire process of creating art. There's also an element of holding on, attempting to master a technique to control the intended expression.

Finding that place inside me where I'm holding on and letting go makes for better pots, I believe. It's possible to hold on to the thought of a lost pot or a broken bowl, but at the same time, I have to let it go. Perhaps I will never discover that space, that perfect point where holding on and letting go coexist. Maybe that's just an ideal to help me adapt and survive. Art is never clear until you make it, and even then, it's always wanting more.

Differences between a Poem and a Pot

Pots weigh more than poems.
It's more difficult to memorize pots.
A poem will not explode if heated too rapidly.

Books

Books are objects that act as three-dimensional transportation devices. I worked in libraries and bookstores through high school, college, and post-college; part of the attraction is to simply look at books all lined up on shelves, to pull a book down and then place it back, moving a book from shelf to shelf, finding a book to purchase, taking it home and placing it on a table next to my bed.

Books are one of the most active art-objects we use. A coffee mug gets a lot of action, but not as much as a book. Books require concentration and imagination, the ability to hold simultaneous thoughts and understand a larger message. Digital books are different, but they achieve the same end. However, the physical object of the book creates a presence in my life. The very fact that physical books take up space is part of their charm. My books on my bookshelf tell me where I've been, what I've read and whom I haven't read because not all the books on my shelves have been read. In that sense, these books on my bookshelf point to places in my past and to places in my future.

I like to think that my paperback copy of Herman Melville's *Moby Dick* showed great patience with me over the years, biding its time for me to get over my prejudices, open my mind and discover its richness. Books are like stars billions of years in the future beaming their light, waiting for that moment when I look up at the night sky and see them flickering at me in the dark.

What?

I am beginning to believe there is no satisfactory answer to that question, but it helps to consider the issue in order to move forward with my work.

My strength as an artist is that I invest all my passion and love into my pots. My weakness lies with the technical, dealing with the issues of craft: attention to detail, finishing and sturdiness. I grow quickly impatient when throwing pots. In the rush to express myself, I take shortcuts. I improvise when I'm lost and making a bad pot; as much as I dread that moment, I also like it because I'm engaged in a type of survival, not just of me, but, say, of a lid on a jar. My pots are full of feeling. My hands constantly move when I'm building pots, my mind making decision after decision in quickening speed. The rhythm is addictive. Who has time to go back and be perfect?

But to make a beautiful pot, there needs to be a synthesis of both feeling and craft. Well-crafted pots can be dull and lifeless despite all the attention to detail if the user cannot feel the human struggle and grace behind them. A beautiful pot connects the maker and the audience in a particular moment of discovery. And often I feel that moment can't be scripted or planned; time and space conspire to convene the moment when your heart has a direct conduit to your hands.

Chaos

I deal with chaos and disorder every time I sit down to work, so in a larger view, creativity is just a way to bring order to the universe. One wants a type of control, a skill and mastery to bring elements together, but I'm not that type of person. I believe the chaos is important to embrace. I'm somebody who admires control, but I don't want too much control in my work.

For example, I've always had a difficult relationship with plot, the mechanics of telling a story. There's a beauty in watching a story unfold, the building of suspense, the deepening of relationships with characters through action and experience. Telling a story requires a lot of control—knowing the elements and "ordering" them in a particular way.

When I became a widower and returned to writing, I realized it was impossible for me to tell a story in a straightforward, linear fashion. My mind is altered; my brain distorted. The pieces of my life appear like shards of clay. I know I could never write a story with a plot. It seems to me that plot is a contrivance. Experience unfolds differently.

Museum

Everywhere I go, I am looking for pots. I am at The Brooklyn Museum and searching their collection of ceramics. I am visiting old friends from our time in New York, recalling the afternoon when Julia and I came upon this same teapot back when we moved to Brooklyn, a pot made by an unknown potter around the turn of the century. I didn't know what I was looking at back in the 1980s. I didn't know anything about art, and I didn't know anything about pots. I was just looking.

But there it is again, right in front of me, and I recognize this same teapot because of its squared body, bolstered feet, squatted pose, blurring and running green copper glazes that accentuate all the different facets. The potter is unknown, but the teapot remains vibrant, alive, almost lit from within. Staring through museum glass so many years later, I identify with this teapot, feel connected to it, although I don't know why. I take out a small pad of paper and start drawing, writing down some phrases that will help me remember this teapot when I get back to my studio to work.

History

From *The Perry Mirror*, Perry, Kansas, Thursday, March 22, 1923, p. 1.

Two Women Murdered

The southern section of Jefferson County was startled Friday afternoon when the word was flashed over the county that Louis Goetz had shot and killed his wife, Catherine Goetz, and Mrs. Montague, at the Montague home two miles northwest of Newman. After killing the two women, Goetz turned the gun upon himself and inflicted a wound from which it was thought he would die, but he was taken to a Topeka hospital and is reported recovering.

Family trouble, according to reports, was the motive for the killing. Goetz came to this section of the county about three years ago and for a time worked at the John Montague farm. Some time later married Catherine Montague, who had made her home with John Montague for a number of years. After, their marriage trouble developed and the couple separated and Goetz left the county. He returned here several weeks ago and had been staying in the neighborhood and on the day of the murder had been seen talking to his wife in the yard. Some time later he went into the house and it is presumed that the quarrel started again and in a fit of anger killed the two women. It is the belief of some that Mrs. Goetz was killed first when she tried to interfere and prevent the man from killing Mrs. Montague. The two women were lying close together when found and the two small children of Mrs. Montague were close by covered with blood. Goetz admitted the killing and begged those who were first on the scene to kill him. Telephone linemen were working near the scene of the tragedy and heard the shots but it was some time before anyone would enter the house as they feared that Goetz would do harm to anyone who attempted to enter. Mr. Montague was working the field and when he learned of the killing went to his brother Joe Montague, a short distance from his own home. Goetz had threatened the family it is said, and Montague had secured an injunction in the District Court to enjoin Goetz from going near the farm.

The bodies of the two women were taken to Topeka and Monday morning funeral services were held at The Holy Name Church.

Ancestors

The two children described in the news clipping as "covered in blood" were my dad and my aunt. My dad was seven months old; my aunt just three.

The story of their youth was never discussed in our family, never mentioned, even though my dad and Aunt Mary have different last names. It was only later when I was in high school, when my aunt was dying, that I understood there had been a tragedy, a terrible scar, a secret in the family that lay beneath everything wrong with all of us.

Aunt Mary told me that shortly after the murder, her father, my grandfather, was in such a deep state of grief that he could not take care of two infant children. He became an alcoholic and eventually lost the family farm. A terrible drought happened. The land became what is known as a "dust bowl." Aunt Mary was given away to the church in Newman, Kansas where she was raised by nuns in a convent until she became an adult. She joined the Navy and became a nurse. My dad was taken in by an elderly couple who had no children. They lived in a small house in Newman. Aunt Mary and my dad grew up aware of each other but were never together.

I think about John Montague, the widower, and I think of myself, and I feel a connection. It's the grief junkie in me that wonders if somewhere hidden in the world is a clue as to what happened in my life. Tragedy doesn't seem so random when you can share it. I think of the pain John must have felt losing everything in his life, watching everything fall apart. The nuns showed pity for my grandfather and gave him a job eventually. Aunt Mary said she had a memory of him around the convent grounds, telling me, "A sad figure, that was my father." He died an alcoholic, and his story is one of shame, one of grief that could not find a way to survive.

After WWII, when my dad left the military, he entered college in Southern California, never to return to Kansas. He chose to make a new life for himself. He met my mother on a blind date. They got married and lived briefly in Merced, California. Four children came along. Every year, my dad received birthday cards from relatives in Kansas, wanting to know why he wasn't speaking to them, why they never heard from him and what it was that they had done to him to make him act this way.

The letters were never answered. The history erased.

Growing up, I never understood this problem, never questioned why. We were a family without an extended family like relatives and cousins. We were isolated with no past.

Later, I understood why my dad had cut off communication, why he never returned to Kansas, why he never spoke of his life in the Midwest. He figured out that forgetting allows a person some freedom; it buys them some time. What is the point of going back? What does it gain anyone? For him, there was always the malaise of grief in Kansas, the notion of failure, the feeling of shame. The new world in California had no such memory which was why he loved California so, why he always told us we were lucky even though we felt so cursed.

I see my father in a whole new light. I see how difficult it had been for him to come into the world, to be abandoned and then somehow survive. And I think of all the fights and arguments over the years, all the misunderstandings, the yelling and insults. Right now, my late father might be someone who would know exactly how I am feeling and where I am found.

Installation

In the middle of a white room stands a white table about waist-high. Twenty-two unglazed porcelain pots cover the surface of the table. The pots are of different shapes, the surface of the table a skyline of rims and spouts.

The audience enters and stands against the walls, creating an inner stage surrounding the table of pots.

Lights down. Silence.

Lights up. Two women wearing white enter from the audience and approach the table. They don't seem to be able to speak. They have something they need to say to one another. Finally, one of them holds up a pot and flicks a finger against its surface to create a "pinging" sound. One listens, while the other pings. We don't know what they are saying, why they can't speak, or how this will end.

Truth

So much time is wasted with untruths, and time is something I feel is running out. One morning, I wake up and make a pact with myself to tell the truth for an entire day. No varnishing, no lies, just truth. All day long. No exceptions. Can I do it? I'm not feeling hopeful. That morning, friends from the community of my small town, Heidi and Roger, invite me over for dinner. I agree to come even though I know it is a bad idea. So there is my first lie, not even ten in the morning.

"Would you like a glass of wine?" asks Heidi. She and her husband Roger live in the over-55 development on the south side of town. They are retirees who love art and had met Julia when she was selling her work at the local art alliance. "By sixty-five," says Heidi, "you're bound to have lost something: a parent, a sibling, a child, a kidney. I am so sorry about your wife."

I remember running into Roger just after Julia died. I was retrieving my mail from the post office, hoping not to see anyone, much less have a deep conversation. Roger took me aside and told me how sad he was to hear the news about Julia's death.

"But maybe you'll understand better now," he said to me there in the lobby of the post office. "Especially after all you've been through." He rested his hand on my shoulder. "Every morning after my first wife died, I would wake up and see time, right in front of me."

My brain was buzzed. I had been drinking in the pub. "What?" I asked Roger.

"Time," he said. "Time moving through me."

I made a note to myself as I was trying to understand Roger: The most normal moments have the potential to be the most life-altering. Grief makes the most normal moments feel both epic and mundane.

"You know what time looks like?" asked Roger. I didn't know why I was having such a hard time understanding him. "Like a cloud, he said. "A big, puffy cloud, moving right through you."

I recall that conversation when I'm introduced to their neighbor, Annie. She is a widow, a friend of Heidi's. "You might have something in common," says Heidi.

Annie is a retired schoolteacher; her husband had been a pilot. We are sitting around their living room table sharing food as I'm attempting to explain to them that an email address isn't like a postal address; each person can have their own email box.

I am having a moment where I suddenly don't understand how I got to where I am, how I am sitting in a townhouse-condo inside a retirement village drinking wine and flirting with a woman in her sixties. It's not as if I'm having a bad time; I'm enjoying sitting inside someone's house and listening to stories.

After dinner, I say goodbye to Heidi and Roger and Annie.

I have to learn to say no to some things when they are offered to me. I need to stop hurling myself so randomly into the world, and stop and think.

Summer approaches. I should be making plans, I should be thinking of some place to go, but all I can think about is going home and making more pots. All I want to do is work. And even though I have never been that type of person who works all the time, there is nothing else in my life now except work. Making pots, as strange as it may seem, is the only thing I look forward to.

I drive home in the dark. I struggle with driving, especially at night. I tell myself that I am fine to drive because I have to tell myself that lie if I want to get around.

Defects

Understanding glaze chemistry feels like reading a detective novel. Everything is a clue, and you can only guess what exactly happened, what event precipitated this effect. When a glaze and a clay body in a pot are fired, the two join together. If everything works right, the glaze is seen as a "good fit" to the clay. However, often there are problems with glaze chemistry, bizarre curiosities, random expressions when heat and time conspire.

Pinholing: an effect on the surface of the glaze, often thought of as a defect because the surface is inconsistent; holes the size of pins burrow inside the glaze surface and make it appear as if something went really wrong with the glaze. Usually, I don't know why the glaze is pinholing. There are so many reasons. Sometimes I try to talk myself into thinking the pinholes are fine. The pinholes give the pot character. I try that and I always come back to my original feeling that something looks wrong with pinholing, as if something within the pot has eaten something disagreeable.

Crawling: when the glaze is applied incorrectly, the glaze will retreat from itself and make a little mountain. Crawling means there is a misunderstanding. It's impossible to comprehend the impulse that made us burst into the world. That is the first question that's never answered, but we live with it.

Shivering: when the glaze flakes off because of the incompatibility between the clay body and the glaze. Solution? Add about five percent Feldspar to make a better fit. I think to myself: when will this be over? How long am I supposed to live in a state of grief? I keep doing all the right things, making pots, taking walks, making new friends, finding a new path for myself, and yet I still feel sad. No matter what I do, I can't escape.

Blistering: a bubbled acned surface, like a terrible skin rash. But there are decorative bloats and blisters that some potters use, and I admire taking a defect and making that defect into art. In the meantime, I don't remember what it was like to live without terrible grief. I want to return to those days, but now I can barely conjure what those days might have been like. That world feels inextricably gone, and no matter how much I dream of lifting this grief off my shoulders, I know it can't be done. Not if I'm being honest with myself. It can only work if I learn to lie to myself, but I can't do that. I won't do that.

Community

There is a roadside memorial in our town that is unofficial and makeshift. Flowers appear out of nowhere on a road where the body of a twelve-year-old girl has been discovered. She was kidnapped, killed, and then abandoned and stashed by the side of the road. Her body is identified, and her story becomes infamous. Pictures of her flash all over the world. Her killer is arrested. The local and national news broadcasts the story about her and the man who stole her life. The makeshift memorial, the constant display of flowers on a nondescript access road, goes on for years and years. People hear of the makeshift memorial in our town and make pilgrimages to honor the girl's memory. Strangers leave tributes. Prayer cards. Candles. Red hearts. Written messages. There is a strange energy that emanates from this scrubby lot of weeds that would otherwise be unmemorable.

Recently, some of the locals have become uncomfortable with having our town associated with such a horrible memory. Most agree they are tired of the makeshift memorial. They are tired of seeing it every time they pass that road to fill up their tanks at the gas station. They are tired of wondering when the memorial will go away, when the wound will heal. They are tired of conjuring up the image of the girl's body as it lay in the bushes for days while a countywide search ensued. They are tired of identifying with a young girl who was just sleeping in her bed when an unknown man kidnapped her, killed her, and then dumped her body. They are tired of standing at their windows and looking out onto their yards and wondering if they are safe. They wish these thoughts would go away. The world is awful. The world is cruel. They know this. They don't need a constant reminder. They have had enough of the makeshift memorial. They have had enough of their own lives.

Eventually, the county arrives and clears away the flowers and the tributes. The job is given to that city agency that deals with dumped trash or abandoned vehicles. As the mayor said: Everyone is doing their job and doing them the best they can.

San Diego

The breakfast comes complimentary at the Hampton Inn. Even though we witness with our own eyes the hotel clerk pulling the food from refrigerated boxes underneath the counter, we pretend to be blind and numb to the microwaved cardboard blandness and the high-intensity sugar rushes that come from a breakfast of waffles, scrambled eggs, English muffins, bagels, cereal, orange juice, and coffee served on Styrofoam plates and eaten with plastic utensils.

"I want to make pots for the Hampton Inn," I say to K who sits across from me in an empty breakfast pavilion in the lobby of our motel. I'm joking, but I'm sort of not joking. I'm feeling inspired right now to go back home and make a dinnerware set for travelers at the Hampton Inn.

K isn't happy that we're in a rush and, therefore, rapidly eating freeze-dried cinnamon rolls before we head to the airport. I can see her mind is elsewhere. She is here on a business trip, and I have driven south to spend a few days with her at her hotel. She has two college-aged kids living with her, so our time together is intermittent. Our relationship has been a secret from her family, something she said she didn't want to deal with along with everything else, and I agreed. But now, she wants me to meet her grown-up children, to get closer to her life, and this is a step that I cannot take. As much as I want to, I'm not ready. K understands me, she knows that my reticence is not because of my heart but because of my fear.

Now the trip is over. Her flight leaves in two hours, but there is stress, and that is something you learn when you spend time traveling with someone; you learn the stress points. You learn that love is wonderful and great, but that people have differences, and that it's rare to find a combination that works.

"Instead of throwing everything into a garbage can," I say, "they can wash the dish and cup and then reuse them."

K understands that this is just me talking, me thinking out loud, me floating words and ideas into the universe willy-nilly, me nervous about getting her to the airport on time, me guilty for causing us to be late getting started, me delaying us downstairs for the complimentary breakfast, me getting K to the airport, me getting her on a plane. And me feeling this moment and understanding that our time together is coming to a close, and holding on to her this morning, grateful to K for bringing me back into my body, into touch, to spend time with our bodies together and how much that means to me and how sorry I am that this feeling between us can no longer endure. The grief has worn off, for her. She wants a regular boyfriend, a real partner. Someone not addicted to grief.

Me, I'm talking nonstop on the freeway, worried about the wildfires, worried that I'm not sure how I can make it there and sell pots when no one wants to travel, worried that the smoke is causing damage to my lungs, and seeing K listening to me, always sympathetic, but also knowing how to take care of herself. I can see how she is coming to her own power, shedding her skin and finding her own way.

"Don't worry," K says to me. "You'll figure it out. You will."

The morning winter light in San Diego is one of the brightest lights I've ever experienced. It's a desert light mixed with the glare of the ocean. My eyes are sensitive, but the reflection from the water and the dry thinness of the air make it sometimes hard to see, even wearing sunglasses. I drop her off at the curb in front of her airline. She will have plenty of time to make her flight. We say goodbye. She promises to text me when she gets home so I don't worry.

I find the freeway and start driving. I need the feeling I get at the beginning of a road trip, the time spent between spaces, hours and hours of being in transit. I am about to drive ten hours north, straight through the middle of the state. Anything can happen on a road trip. Maybe nothing will happen at all, and I'll just listen to the radio. Maybe I'll run out of gas. Maybe I won't. Whatever happens or doesn't happen doesn't matter. I'm not clear where I belong in this world, a fact I have to get used to and become comfortable with because I can't envision sharing my life with anyone. The paradox in me is this need to feel belonged, but also my drive to find my own way to make art which can't comply with the usual modes. What soothes me right now is being alone and heading back to my studio to work, to make some more pots, and now dreaming of an art installation, about this set of pots I was thinking about during breakfast, to create a room much like the lobby of the Hampton Inn and to display a set of place settings for twenty travelers who are in the middle of a journey, far from home but not close to their destination, a place on the road called the in-between. Something like that.

Attachments

When you make a mug, you must also make a handle (unless it's a handleless mug). Whenever you join two pieces together, like a handle to a cup, that piece where the two conjoin is a place of vulnerability because until the clay is fired into a solid state, the attachments are in a perilous position. The handle may look attached to the teapot, but until it's fired, it's just an illusion that the teapot and the handle are one and the same.

More often than not, when I'm working in the studio and I check in on my pots, I'll discover an attachment falling off or looking close to falling off. I spend a lot of time chasing cracks and rubbing the surface of the clay with a plastic rib. It's like being an encourager, a negotiator, a last-minute hope to bring the two pieces together. And the more pots I make, the better I get at this skill. Like with everything, two separate pieces joined together will adhere to one another more faithfully if dried together over a long period of time.

Feeling unattached becomes a type of emptiness in the world. A lot of the problems in the world come from people who are unloved and unseen. Of course, unloved people can thrive and have interesting lives, but they will feel an emptiness inside them.

I can't get attached to anything in my life, except pots. Everything is temporary. The fear of being attached is more accurately described as the fear of the attachment breaking off. When a handle on a glazed and fired cup breaks off (and they do after a lot of wear and tear), it's possible to glue the handle back to the cup, but the attachment is cosmetic. The handle can't be used. And that notion is the fear inside me, of losing all over again, of falling off and losing the person you've loved.

There are many workarounds. For example, the solution to attachments with clay is to exclusively make tea bowls and handle-less cups.

Dock

Inside a dormitory built over an inlet of water along the coast of Maine, I struggle to sleep. You would think the idyllic nighttime theater of lapping waves would lull one to sleep without effort. Outside the window, the moon reflects on the water, shadowed profiles of moored boats in the distance bobbing up and down. I am taking a workshop on making functional pots, living in a dorm, and struggling with sobriety.

My body attempts to keep up with the workshop, making lots of pots and firing kilns in a highly intensive manner. My brain trips all around me, absorbing this world of pots and learning new skills, flooded with all the pots I'm seeing in the workshop, everything I'm learning about what makes a good pot. It's like pottery camp, but for people serious about pots. And all the eagerness for pots makes it harder to sleep.

Tonight is the last night of the workshop session, and despite the excitement, I feel a wave of anxiety coming over me thinking about returning to my life. I have said my goodbyes and gone to bed, but most of the school continues to party. It is a warm night. They are shedding their clothes, swimming in the ocean, finding the coves with phosphorescence, drinking, dancing. The evening gets warmer. I close my mind and the wheel turns; I'm thinking about my pots that came out of the salt kiln.

From my window, I overhear a group sitting on the bench next to the dock. The water carries their voices through my window of the dormitory. I smell a cigarette. I hear laughter. The water is too cold by the pier; you need to walk out about a half a mile and jump from a rock. We never understand what we have in our lives, never fully grasp all the beauty in these moments. But I am here now, I am listening, and I am appreciating from afar.

Then the voices dissipate and the quiet returns. The partygoers return to the campus where there is more dancing, more drinking, more saying goodbye, but the sounds are far away. All I hear is the lapping of the water when I drift off to half-sleep. Slowly, I am awakened by a sound coming from the dock. I open my eyes; the room is dark, and I am alone. The other beds are empty. I hear moaning, a sound of someone in distress.

I recognize the voice as belonging to a young student who is crying, not just weeping but sobbing, over and over again, a desperate flood of gasps and inhales of breath that seem to have no end. I get up and look through the window; I see a young woman sitting alone on the bench, her hands cradling her face.

From the tremor of the voice, I am certain that the woman sitting on the dock underneath the moonlight, crying with all the pain in the world, is named Heather. She is one of the youngest in the pottery class, the one trying the hardest to impress. I'm old enough to be her dad. We've had one or two conversations over the past two weeks, but I don't really know Heather. Earlier in the evening, I noticed she was already drunk. Now, hours later, she is alone and sobbing with a grief that alarms me.

I think maybe I should go down to the dock and check on her. On the other hand, part of me thinks she needs to expel this grief, this crying, this sobbing without end. There are the cries of physical pain and there are the cries of psychic pain, and they are very different. Our sense of survival understands the difference, and her pain is the pain of youth, of expectation and disappointment, acceptance and rejection. I understand how difficult endings can be, and there's a certain part of me that respects her sorrow and doesn't want to quell that sadness.

I go back to bed, lie on my back and stare at the ceiling. The world moves through me as I close my eyes. The walls vibrate with her sobs. I lose track of time listening to her cries, my body chilled from the cold coming off the lapping surface of the water.

Sharing

O ne thing I have learned is that when you get old, people seem to care less and less about you. I only say this anecdotally because during my work in hospice helping other people in my community go through the process of grief, I have come into contact with mostly elderly people who have lost their significant others and who now face the remainder of their lives alone. A lot of the elderly around here live in retirement communities, cut off from the rest of the world and perhaps their own families. It's just as difficult to lose someone you love when you're older as it is when you're younger; in a way, it may be more difficult because you're more vulnerable.

Every two weeks, we meet, and I facilitate the group. In the community room at the senior center, the pain of death is palpable, and there is a lot of crying. A woman in our group whose father passed away says she can barely function even though she is a working mother and a wife. There is a man in our group whose wife died as he drove her to the hospital for what they believed to be an allergic reaction. Every town has its own grief, but most of it is hidden. I'm always amazed at how just forming a group, telling stories, and making space collectively can improve our understanding of ourselves.

One of the principles of this type of grief support is to be a listener, and that means that as a facilitator, you never share your own story of grief. In other words, you sit and listen and don't compare. You avoid the distraction. You're not a psychologist. You're not a doctor. You don't have any judgments at all. You simply listen, and it's a wonderful thing to do for someone who is in psychological and emotional pain.

During one of our meeting-sessions, a woman who co-facilitates the group with me breaks that rule and begins to tell the story of how she lost her son when he was seventeen years old. Soon, she is sobbing and crying and reaching for the box of tissues. I feel more upset that she violated that rule than I do about the death of her teenage son because now I am the only one in the group who hasn't shared my own story of grief, and I didn't want to share that story right now. I realize I'm getting tired of sharing my story of grief.

"What about you?" asks the working mother. "What happened to you?"

I decide not to share my story tonight, but the dynamic in the group has changed.

At the next meeting, I am alone inside the senior center, setting up the chairs and bringing out a tray; everyone brings something to eat, something to snack on. The days are getting shorter, and the holidays approach with their usual intensity. I'm feeling tired and exhausted, the same way I felt when I realized my teaching career was over, when my student answered her cellphone in the middle of her presentation; I am feeling that same dread in the pit of my stomach, that same uneasiness. It is around this time that I have ceased feeling that adrenaline rush that occurs when I come into contact with grief. Something in me has begun to fade, and the thought of going to one of these meetings, let alone running one of these meetings, depresses me and makes me sad.

At the beginning of our grief support group, we sit down in a circle and face our chairs toward the center. I tell the group I don't want to share my story of grief for my own private reasons, but I also tell them I think that I've been hiding from the world inside my grief, that grief has been a potent shield against the fears I have of living in the world at large.

There is silence. No one knows what I'm talking about.

I tell them that I am surprised at myself, how clever I have been, how I have done whatever I could do to survive even by hiding my own strategy from myself. But now I am tired of grief, and tired of hiding behind it.

Reduction

I don't consider myself a person who invites melodrama. For the most part, I appear calm and take things in stride. I don't like to be the center of attention. But I am having dreams, lots of dreams every night, and these dreams will not go away. I dream of watching my friends visit me and then drive away in a convertible car; they cross the road as the river starts to rise and fill the interior. I watch the car flood and my friends swim to shore. I have dreams about being asleep and waking to the sound of a truck driving over me. The dreams won't stop. I know what they mean, but they are coming more frequently and with greater intensity.

I take these constant nightmares as just part of who I am, an effect of trauma, as part of the regimen of how I survive. My subconscious carries me back to the bend in the river where Julia died. How can I make the nightmares stop? My only idea is to face the nightmare and to visit this place that haunts me. On my birthday, I decide to take a ride out to the coast. I want to see the ocean, but I am also anxious. I don't know what I'm going to do out there, but I'm going to drive, and when I drive, I will navigate past the location where Julia drowned. I am going to force myself to do this because the idea of it frightens me so much and sickens me so much that if I don't face this fear, if I spend the rest of my life avoiding this patch of earth, I'm only going to feel more afraid.

So I drive and I think to myself how sad it is to drive on my birthday past the place where Julia died. And I think to myself, how long will this grief live inside me? How can I get the grief to end? What can I do? Here I am on the two-lane highway that snakes along the Navarro River. Driving this stretch of highway is mostly under the canopy of redwoods, the light throwing shadows. The beauty overwhelms me, makes me recall how much Julia and I had loved this area of the world and how we had been making plans to move here, to the coast, and to build a life. I know the mile marker where Julia died, and I count them as my car winds north and west, where the dryness of the valley begins to mix with the dew of the redwoods and the salt from the ocean. I am driving, numb but aware of myself, when I come to the mile marker, the river opening up to the ocean, and the fog drifting over the rocky cliffs. This is the place where she lost control of the truck and fell down the riverbank.

There's no spot to pull out; the traffic moves towards an intersection where the road meets the coast highway which is busy with tourists driving toward Mendocino. Part of me leaves my body, but my Toyota keeps driving, and I come to the intersection where I can go north or south. Out of an old habit, I go south along the coast toward the town of Elk. And I've done it, I've made it past the bend in the river where Julia left this world, and now I am here on the coast once again. It's not just the reminder of the night she died but also the return to this geography, feeling the warmth of this rocky coast, the thick fog, the monument-like cliffs.

The scenery conjures memories I have forced myself to forget, but they are good memories, feelings of spending time out here together, the good thoughts outweighing the bad memories. We would drive out here two or three times a month in our van with our dog, camp at the ocean, and Julia would work the day in the craft gallery as part of the artist's cooperative. I'd take our dog on long walks, and in the evening, before we drove back, we'd stop at a little inn and order dinner where I ate chicken pot pie.

When I arrive in the town of Elk, I see it is exactly the same. I spot the gallery where Julia showed her work and where she gallery-sat the last day of her life. I hadn't meant to visit Elk, but I'm glad I ended up here. Part of me is looking for that place where I ate chicken pot pie, and so I stop the car. The town is perched high over a cliff, a string of small houses, an old schoolhouse, horse barns, a few small inns, a gift shop, an automobile garage, and a massage therapist. On the cliffs, the trails run through dry grass looking out over the Pacific. Some days you can see whales, but most days are gray with sun sometimes peeking through. I see an image of us flying a kite together, our dog barking at the kite. The beach sits down at the bottom of a long steep trail, a perfect crescent beach, and so I walk down to the beach under the leaning arms of Monterey cypress. I feel under a type of hypnosis, in a dream world. I am here in the village of Elk, and I feel as if I had been drawn here, not of my own volition.

There is also the expanse of relief getting past that part in the river, of being near it, looking at it and facing its truth. I pace up and down the ocean's edge, and I know somewhere beyond me, beyond these waters, swim pods of whales. I don't have to see them to know they are there. As the sun emerges, I think to myself what Julia's last day on this earth was like. I recall how she worked in the gallery, an old house that a group of artists converted into a gallery. In the kitchen area of the house, Julia displayed her ceramics. I haven't thought of these memories in years.

And then I recall the gallery has a log, a diary written by all the artists in the collective about what they saw or observed during their gallery-sitting. Sometimes they drew a picture. Sometimes they described the sales. Often, someone would have a suggestion.

I know instantly that Julia wrote inside that book on the last day of her life. I know for certain that inside that journal-log she would have made an entry, or she would have drawn a picture—her last expression before she drove home to make dinner for me.

I walk across the highway and enter the front door. It is a moment that I never thought I would encounter, to come back to this gallery and to walk inside. I recognize the artist behind the desk; he is one of the members who works with wood. His name is Ribani. I tell him who I am, and then he recognizes me. It is good to see him again. The family of artists here were very close to Julia. When she died, it was too painful to be in contact with them, but I remember all of them. I tell him about the thought I had down on the beach. I wonder if they kept the old journals? He says he'll take a look. After a few minutes, he emerges from the back storage room with a book: Artists Notebook.

Ribani leaves me alone as I scan the pages and find the date of Julia's death. There is her entry, in her handwriting. The words jump off the page. It's like confronting Julia all over again, coming into her presence and finding a bit of her, this paragraph, this last expression before the tide of forgetting and erasure.

A sketch of a teapot.

I find my phone and take a picture. I read it again. Unsteady, I look around the gallery, this house full of art.

Nature

Firing a kiln is like running a half marathon even though I'm mostly standing around staring at it and worrying. The pots inside the kiln represent over a month's worth of time and energy. The kiln is nothing more than a brick chamber stacked with shelves balancing cups and bowls, platters and teapots. Eight burners underneath the kiln send flame upwards into the enclosure. Preparing, loading, and firing a kiln takes stamina and energy. In my care lay the fate of roughly seventy-five pots that I have promised to take on a journey over the course of twelve hours to upwards of 2370 Fahrenheit.

The winds kick up, and the power flickers. The previous night I fired a kiln off at three in the morning, rose early to clean up around the kiln, and worked at the farmer's market to sell my pots. My feet are tired from working on a cement kiln pad, selling pots in the parking lot behind the town square—my knees and hips exhausted from standing, waiting and talking.

This evening I plan to recuperate, but at midnight the winds pound harder against the walls of my cabin. A powerful storm approaches. I am distracted, however, picturing those pots cooling in the kiln, imagining how the glazes have matured from the firing as the day progressed, and what these pots might look like when I open the kiln the following day. There is nothing in my power I can do at this moment to change or help the pots in my kiln. The only thing I can do is wait.

I live alone at the end of a remote road in mountains covered with dry oak and parched pine, scrubby bushes, dried-out ditches and creek beds. The trees twist and moan from the gusts of wind. I should be more concerned, but I am too tired, too love-sick over pots I wait to greet the following morning. What I really want is sleep. I close all the windows in my cabin so I won't be woken by the sound of gusting winds, and shortly afterwards I fall into bed.

At four in the morning, the county sheriff knocks the butt of his flashlight against my front door, flashing red and blue lights, a siren, a loudspeaker informing me that a wildfire quickly approaches, ordering me to evacuate immediately.

The power is out, and my cabin is dark. I roll over and get out of bed, dazed.

The sheriff shouts: *There is no emergency backup. No fire trucks are coming. The hospitals are evacuated. The time to leave is now.*

The night skies are charcoal except for an orange glow pulsing from behind the ridgetop.

The sheriff returns to his vehicle and makes a U-turn, the sound of his booming voice echoing down the hill.

The image triggers me.

This isn't happening, I think to myself, but I know I'm wrong. I know denial won't work. I can see the flame behind the cellphone tower; I can feel the energy moving toward me, ready to consume. How insignificant I feel at this moment, how unborn my life remains in comparison to the tower of flames moving toward me, my studio, and my pots.

Evacuate

Intense heat creates its own micro-climate. Winds blow with hurricane-like force overhead, limbs from trees strewn across the road. I return inside, put on a pair of jeans, a t-shirt and a sweatshirt, and search for a pair of clean socks. There is no electrical power, no hum from the refrigerator—the quiet of disaster. My mind unfolds in a controlled panic, racing in several directions simultaneously. I tie my shoes, slowly and deliberately; I don't want to trip and fall. That is the number one thing because it is dark and I can't locate my flashlight. The smoke becomes intense. I reach for my phone and my computer. I grab a handful of clothes and stuff them into a paper bag. What else do I need?

I step out of my own skin, watching myself from a ghostly post, calmly taking notes on myself and my own actions. There I am grabbing more clothes, my passport, some cash, and a bottle of water. I am doing what I am supposed to do and leaving quickly. How much time passes? I feel something familiar flowing through me: a grief, an anticipation of loss, an acceptance of the inevitable. It's adrenaline flooding my veins. I've never stopped feeling this adrenaline. A wall of fire threatens to overtake the ridge and burn the ground beneath me, and I'm getting a rush, the anticipation of grief.

It's happening again, I think to myself.

The air thickens with smoke as the winds continue to blow westward. I walk quickly to my car. Running seems like something a panicked person would do. The only way out is to drive down the ridge and across the river. I have no idea where the fire is burning, but it is beginning to feel as if the fire burns right behind me in an area of several hundred uninhabited acres of fuel.

It's happening again. I can feel it in my neck.

I turn the ignition and put my car in gear, but I hesitate. I can't simply drive away. I have water hoses around the cabin and studio. I get out of my Toyota, walk back to the studio and start watering the roof and sides. The smoke thickens, making it hard to see down the road. The orange glow becomes brighter. It's getting harder to breathe. I have to let go, but I am not ready to let go. I can't accept the finality of the moment, but there isn't a choice. More than anything, I want to survive.

I hurry into the studio. Even though it is dark, I know the interior of that studio like I know my own hand. Next to my wheel, I keep a mug made by Julia. Of all the pots I own, I cannot leave without this curved brown mug. I tuck it safely into the space below the driver's seat. My goal is to make it down the mountain and across the river, but the atmosphere is eerily quiet, as if I have fallen into the center of a storm. There isn't time to absorb the enormity of the moment. The sweep of light from the headlights on my car illuminates the dust and smoke billowing in the driveway. As I leave, I lean out the window and take a flash picture with my phone, a last-minute gesture to hold onto what is about to disappear.

Flame

All I can see is flame in the rearview mirror as I evacuate down the mountain. The orange glow on the other side of the hill becomes brighter. I follow the road, my mouth covered with a studio towel. I'm not sure what will happen next. I use my blinker to indicate to no one that I'm turning left. Following rules is like some sort of disease in me that I can never shake. I cross the single-lane bridge, drive over a dirt road and up to the access road. Now I am safe. My car becomes my life raft in an ocean of fire. My neighbors have parked on the other side of the river, outlines of bodies standing outside of their cars, talking on cellphones and looking up at the mountain. I keep doubting what is happening, but their pale faces staring up the ridgeline is my proof.

But instead of stopping, I keep driving. I steer away from the wildfires, as if I am simply driving into our small town to pick up supplies, to have a cup of coffee and perhaps take a walk. But I am pretending. I am using make-believe to calm myself. The winds are blowing up to forty miles an hour, and the earth has turned dark. Debris blows across the farm roads, and garbage cans turn upside down and fall sideways. The small town outside where I live sits abandoned: empty stores, no traffic lights, no neon. I spot two figures walking near the cinema theater. When I stop them, I recognize my neighbors, Doby and Tom. I ask what they are doing, and they reply, "Wandering around in the dark." I am hoping they are being sarcastic, hoping there is some humor in this situation, but there isn't any humor.

I park my car, thinking it is better to be with them than alone. We walk to the police station and talk to the dispatcher through plated glass. It is then that I learn the scope of the event. The fire will be arriving in thirty minutes on the outskirts of town or farther south depending on the wind's direction.

The matter-of-factness stuns me. The information has no emotional transport except the weight of its own implications. The fire is like a train on a schedule, reliable and predictable, as if we are consulting a table of times for destruction's entrance. We are advised to gather at the evacuation center down at the fairgrounds and wait.

Disaster isn't always hysterical; it can sometimes be as plain as a wind blowing north or a wind blowing south. We walk back to our cars and drive to the evacuation center. Doby and Tom tell me they lost a house in Oakland a decade ago. I'm in a state of shock; my lips become numb. The highways are closed. People are stranded. There's a moment where I want to take everything back, to rewind and start over again, but I can't do that. I can't stop anything.

We wait underneath the awning at the evacuation center, standing in the breezeway looking up at the fire burning the hillsides. More people arrive, faces in shock, relief, confusion. Car doors open, and persons wearing pajamas and hiking boots walk past us. The warm winds push us off the sidewalks, doors swinging open from gusts blowing off the sides of the ridge. More people arrive looking for answers. We don't know exactly how we got here, so we can't really help.

We sign a clipboard marking ourselves as SAFE. We write our name, our address, our cellphone, and the time we arrived.

Bewilderment

The sun waits to rise over the Mayacamas Mountains. I am standing at the evacuation center, watching families, couples, children, dogs on leashes, a truck with a man sitting in a wheelchair tied to the truck by a rope. Inside the fairgrounds is a gymnasium and clusters of people looking bewildered and numb. A wildfire rages outside the town limits. There are rumors that all of Santa Rosa is burning. As far as I know, the fire has not reached my cabin, but it is difficult to get information.

Here is a place that is both alien and familiar: the unsteadiness that comes from not knowing what is going to happen. It's a psychological space in our normal lives that can sometimes be quickly buried or ignored; but with wildfires and no information, there is nothing that can be done, nothing that can be avoided or suppressed. This is the area of bewilderment. What will happen to my cabin? What will happen to all of us? The only truth is not knowing.

The lights in the breezeway give luminance in the dark. I focus on the details. I see a woman sitting in her car talking on her phone. She must be sixty years old. In the passenger seat sits a St. Bernard whose wide shoulders and fur seem to fill the entire seat. The woman inhales a cigarette and exhales a plume of smoke between the glass and the frame of the door.

I am standing alone now, separated from the others. The winds lessen; they are not as violent but they are unpredictable. Gusts blow the embers and start scattered fires along the ridge. I try to imagine how the scene appears back at the cabin, how the fire might have raced over the creek and up the hill. It's inconceivable to think about losing everything that you have, until you do. It's inconceivable that somehow I thought this wouldn't happen to me, that I'd had enough grief in my life. But that is wrong, and I know it; there is no cap on loss.

The sun rises. The winds quiet and begin to cease. It's not just the breeze but also the change in sound, the howling of the gusts of wind as the skies turn silent.

By ten in the morning, the fires burn, but they are not sweeping towards our town at the rate they were this morning at dawn. Smoke is everywhere, and the sun turns the empty streets and parking lots into sepia film. There are fires all over the county, and most of the resources are being used by Santa Rosa where they are needed most. Helicopters circle overhead, single-engine airplanes coming out of the smoke and then disappearing again.

Remainders

It has been four days since I drove down the mountain, returning to the evacuation center where I spent the following days sleeping in my car and then later staying with friends.

The wildfires continue to burn, but there is some sense of containment. The fires have retreated, lines are being held, the temperatures cooling. In the valley five miles south, just over the ridgeline and along the slopes, the earth is scarred from the path of the fire, blackened, stripped of life. Oak trees stand in profile like iron sculptures, bent and bowed from the force of the heat. I have neighbors who have lost everything they owned. Walking across the landscape, the ground underneath my boots is black. The stench of smoke infiltrates my clothes, the inside of my car. There are no insects. There is no color except gray and black. This is the color of death.

Don't worry, the people say in their hopeful bromides to ward off grief. *Spring will come. The skies will bring rain. The wildflowers will be beautiful. The hills will green themselves.*

Yes, I think, that's a nice way to cope with sadness. But what happened to the animals? What happened to the birds? Why don't we mention them? The animals are gone. They've disappeared.

I drive over the bridge and up the hill, past the campground and the dried-out underbrush. Every living oak tree I pass I imagine bursting into flame. The atmosphere is quiet and still as I drive up the road and park. I creep out of my car and walk toward the studio in a type of disbelief, fearful and, at the same time, hopeful. There is my cabin. There is my studio. The trees and immediate landscape are unscathed, the fire having circled south of my property but never running down the ridge where I see burnt trees.

I fled this scene a few days ago believing I would never see it again. I had begun the process of grief, but I was wrong. My home has survived.

Why didn't the fire burn my way? What stopped the path of the flame from running over my life and consuming it? The answer probably has to do with prevailing winds, but the truth feels more complex. Why is someone saved and someone not? I recognize I am in receipt of a gift, a reprieve. For a reason I will never understand no matter how hard I try, the hand of the universe decided at this moment to save me and to save this studio.

I am alone, standing outside staring at all the pots strewn across the ground. There are no sounds, no winds, no signs of life. It reminds me of the feeling I had shortly after Julia died when I felt like a ghost walking through a life that didn't include me. It's as if I'm witnessing the future minus my own purpose in the world, a preview of what this world will look like without me.

I walk inside the studio and open the windows; everything remains just as I left it. Light pours down from the skylight overhead. There is my wheel, my rack of pots, my tools, my notes and drawings. There is work that I forgot to cover, and it has now dried out. I flip the switch on my wheel to see if there is power and electricity. Yes. I test the faucets and inspect the water. All is fine. I see this art studio in a different light this morning.

What I see is a space transformed, a studio that no longer feels like Julia's studio, but a studio that is my own. I haven't been able to absorb it, but this room, this space, has been the tool that has saved me as much as the indifference of any wildfire. I recall entering this clay studio shortly after becoming a widower—confused, off-balance, intimidated. At times, I've felt afraid while working inside this space, traumatized and unable to escape. I decided at some point to become friends with this ceramic studio, to not run away but to investigate this space, to find my way through it, inch by inch. I've learned how to use all the tools in this studio. I've learned how to use all the raw chemicals and mix them into new chemistries. I've learned how to apply myself in a way that was unknown to me.

I push the studio doors from the studio to the kiln pad. I unlatch the bolt on the kiln, and the door swings open. Behind the bolted kiln-door waits a silent wall of residual heat. Centimeter by centimeter, the door widens.

My pots.

Despite the toils of the firing and the past few days, the pots from my kiln that I fired just before the wildfires remain, all the cups, bowls, vases, and jars standing patiently in rows, mute. All that labor and sweat transformed into poetry, love notes written on the walls of the human heart. I retrieve each pot from the kiln, one at a time, looking at them through filtered, smoky light. Each pot describes the process of the firing by judging the marks on the surface, where the pot sat in the kiln, how it faced the effects of flame.

Everything seems just as it was before the wildfire, but I know nothing is ever the same. A few flowerpots had tipped over on my deck. A coat of ash covers the railings. The windstorm had tossed my empty garbage bins down the hill into the gulch. There are minor cuts and bruises. I'm relieved and anxious.

There is celebration when opening a kiln, especially one that survives a wildfire, but there is an aura of grief that surrounds me today, a grief that is impossible to ignore of a growing climate crisis, the death of nature, the diminishment of resources, the scars of overdevelopment and overpopulation. There is not much time left. We know this fact. The air reeks of it.

Still, time is moving forward, and there is a lot to do right now: the unloading of the kiln, the cleaning of the pots, the resetting of the studio to create another cycle of work. I turn on the radio and listen to music. I have this feeling that no matter what happens to me, no matter what I lose, whether it's my studio or my home and all the pots in it, I can always make new pots, I can always make art.

Syllabus

This workshop will be done in complete silence. No words. No cameras or video allowed. The instructor will demonstrate, and the students will work on their own. Clay as a material is optional. Questions will be raised and answered with work. The skills of silence, concentration, listening, and observation will be emphasized in this "hands-on" workshop.

Metamorphosis

When I begin to write again, I stand in front of a great emptiness. The more I think about it, the worse it gets. When similar thoughts come over me in the clay studio, I feel a *déjà vu*. A bag of clay asks: What will you make of me? What do you need to make? Once again, I can overthink. What can be done when we face freedom? Why is it uncomfortable at times? It shouldn't be. A blank page. A bag of clay. These are invitations to be with ourselves.

I think my whole life I've been searching for a place to write. A space of quiet, a place of no distraction, an environment of simplicity. In my mind there exists some pine desk pushed up against a set of paned windows through which a soft northern light spills over the pages of my writing. Where this space exists, I don't know, but it's an image in my mind, an imaginary space where I always believe I can "write."

Over the years, I've set up writing spaces in closets, storage lockers, nooks and crannies of laundry rooms. I write on trains, buses, or inside bars. I've searched but never found an idyllic place to write. There's always some obstacle, real or imagined, that makes writing hard.

When I write, I have to get inside a bubble of concentration, and perhaps that is the greatest gift of writing—the pursuit of concentration. To sit down, remove myself from the bodily world, and invest my energies in the mechanisms of my natural intelligence. That bubble world of writing is a transportable place; I can take it around the world and open it up wherever I am if the powers of my concentration are that strong.

Working inside the writing bubble can be the most blissful state or the most agonizing. There is the blank space of the page to confront; the mundane world of thinking that circles my bubble and threatens to tear it down; and finally, the sound of my voice against the silence. The faith of the writer brings me to this bubble of creativity and then the writer lets go. All I can do is propel myself in every way to this state of being, this place of writing, this moment of transformation.

Acknowledgments

This book would not have been possible without the support of my friends, my community of writers and artists, and Julia's family. I also want to thank the following institutions and the people who support them for the time and space to write this book: Carrizozo AIR, Carrizozo, New Mexico; Dorland Mountain Arts Colony, Temecula, CA; and Pond Farm Artist Residency, Guerneville, CA.

About the Author

Vince Montague received his Master's Degree in Creative Writing from NYU in 1989 and soon after began publishing short stories in literary magazines. He also began a twenty-year career as an adjunct instructor of writing at colleges and universities around the Bay Area. In 2014, he left his teaching career, reopened his wife's ceramic studio, and began making art for a living.

His stories and poems have been published in literary and academic journals, including: *California Quarterly, Westwind, The Florida Review, Talking River Review, Other Voices, Nimrod: An International Journal, Green Mountain Review.*

CPSIA information can be obtained
at www.ICGtesting.com
Printed in the USA
JSHW082318230123
36681JS00001B/1